PRAISE FOR
FOLLOWING EZRA

"*Following Ezra* is a revelation. I could not put it down. Life rarely goes according to plan, and too often we try to control situations that are beyond our control. In this life-affirming book, Tom Fields-Meyer offers a rare gift: He teaches that the things we least plan for can become our greatest treasures. This inspiring memoir of a father raising (and being raised by) his autistic son is a great lesson about patience and the blessings that can come when we let our unique children lead us."   —Naomi Levy, author of *To Begin Again* and *Hope Will Find You*

"A riveting account of raising one special boy, *Following Ezra* is a powerful story for parents of any child. This inspiring book shows us that seeing meaning and depth in our children's idiosyncrasies is crucial to raising strong, secure, and resilient kids. Tom Fields-Meyer has written a beautiful, funny, tender book. I highly recommend it."

—Michael Gurian, *New York Times* bestselling author of
The Wonder of Boys and *Nurture the Nature*

"In a world with such narrow yet outsized definitions of success, this enchanting and profound book is a reminder that each child is made in God's image. I was sad to reach the last page. I'll miss following the exuberant Ezra."

—Wendy Mogel, PhD, author of *The Blessing of a Skinned Knee*
and *The Blessing of a B Minus*

"I look for love in books about children. I trust the parent who yields to wonder and celebrates the unexpected. I honor the writer who tells a family story with dignity, clarity, and grace. Love is the river that runs through this book. Dignity and grace light each page."

—Beth Kephart, National Book Award finalist
for *A Slant of Sun* and author of *Undercover*

continued . . .

"Anyone who is raising a child with special needs should read *Following Ezra*. It shows how warmth and humor—yes, humor—can help not just the child, but the family, more than most of us could ever imagine."

—James Patterson, *New York Times* bestselling author

"*Following Ezra* is an unsentimental, beautifully written memoir about a boy whose limitations and gifts are as extraordinary as his impact on the reader's life. Like Ezra himself, this book is by turns funny, painful, poignant, and scrupulously honest."

—David J. Wolpe, author of *Why Faith Matters*

"When Tom Fields-Meyer's son Ezra was diagnosed with autism, the author decided to forgo mourning for the child who might have been, and concentrate instead on the delightful kid he had. *Following Ezra* is at once a meticulous description of what it is to parent a child who has autism and a salute to the kid whose mind takes both of them to mysterious, profound, and silly places we so-called typical adults can scarcely imagine."

—Carolyn See, author of *Making a Literary Life* and grandmother of a child with autism

"The moving, fascinating story of a father's journey toward understanding and hope." —Daniel Tammet, *New York Times* bestselling author of *Born on a Blue Day*

"*Following Ezra* offers a moving testimony to the strength and breadth of the human spirit. Tom Fields-Meyer provides a tale that transcends the fears and challenges of raising his autistic son, and shares how Ezra teaches him to appreciate the beauty and depth of the world in surprising and unanticipated ways. In so doing, Fields-Meyer expands our humanity and demonstrates that love and connection are possible in ways we might not have imagined—if only we are open. I laughed and I cried as I read page after page of this poignant, powerful, inspiring, and gentle book."

—David Ellenson, president, Hebrew Union College–Jewish Institute of Religion

"*Following Ezra* is a revealing and poignant memoir, told with deep reflection and insight. We feel the fear of the unknown, the peace of acceptance, the exhilaration of hope, and the endurance of love as father and son discover each other and find their way. It will bring help and inspiration to all those who wear these shoes, and enlighten all parents to celebrate the uniqueness of their children."

—Ricki G. Robinson, MD, MPH, author of
Autism Solutions: How to Create a Healthy and Meaningful Life for Your Child

"Follow extraordinary father and gifted writer Tom Fields-Meyer as he walks with his special son, Ezra. Ezra's struggles to live life fully and to be a participant in his beautiful family and the larger world will fill your heart and inspire you in your own challenges. His sweetness, courage, and resilience come alive in his father's watchful gaze and masterful portrayal. Reading this book makes you feel like you just gained a new set of relatives—wise, sometimes goofy, always remarkable."

—Bradley Shavit Artson, dean, Ziegler School of Rabbinic Studies
and author of *The Everyday Torah*

"A book about autism isn't supposed to be funny. But I laughed reading *Following Ezra* as much as I cried. There's sadness here, but also great joy, boundless love, and inspiring devotion. Ezra teaches not only his father, but all of us—about our foibles, our silliness, our narrowness, and our capacity to grow, to learn, and to love. And in doing that, following Ezra—and reading his story—makes us better people. This book is a great and uplifting gift."

—Daniel Gordis, author of *Saving Israel* and *Coming Together, Coming Apart*

"A spot-on memoir that becomes positively transcendent as we follow sweet, worried, joyful Ezra from childhood into early adolescence and the preparations for his bar mitzvah. This story will illuminate the experience of parenting a child with autism for those who don't know it and will resonate with those of us who know it all too well. There are blessings along the way, and Tom Fields-Meyer depicts them beautifully." —Cammie McGovern, author of *Eye Contact* and *Neighborhood Watch*

FOLLOWING EZRA

**What One Father Learned About
Gumby, Otters, Autism, and Love
from His Extraordinary Son**

Tom Fields-Meyer

NEW AMERICAN LIBRARY

New American Library
Published by New American Library, a division of
Penguin Group (USA) Inc., 375 Hudson Street,
New York, New York 10014, USA
Penguin Group (Canada), 90 Eglinton Avenue East, Suite 700, Toronto,
Ontario M4P 2Y3, Canada (a division of Pearson Penguin Canada Inc.)
Penguin Books Ltd., 80 Strand, London WC2R 0RL, England
Penguin Ireland, 25 St. Stephen's Green, Dublin 2,
Ireland (a division of Penguin Books Ltd.)
Penguin Group (Australia), 250 Camberwell Road, Camberwell, Victoria 3124,
Australia (a division of Pearson Australia Group Pty. Ltd.)
Penguin Books India Pvt. Ltd., 11 Community Centre, Panchsheel Park,
New Delhi - 110 017, India
Penguin Group (NZ), 67 Apollo Drive, Rosedale, Auckland 0632,
New Zealand (a division of Pearson New Zealand Ltd.)
Penguin Books (South Africa) (Pty.) Ltd., 24 Sturdee Avenue,
Rosebank, Johannesburg 2196, South Africa

Penguin Books Ltd., Registered Offices:
80 Strand, London WC2R 0RL, England

First published by New American Library,
a division of Penguin Group (USA) Inc.

First Printing, September 2011
10 9 8 7 6 5 4 3

 REGISTERED TRADEMARK—MARCA REGISTRADA

LIBRARY OF CONGRESS CATALOGING-IN-PUBLICATION DATA:

Fields-Meyer, Thomas.
Following Ezra: what one father learned about Gumby, Otters, autism, and love from his extraordinary son/Tom
Fields-Meyer.
    p. cm.
  ISBN 978-0-451-23463-6
  1. Fields-Meyer, Thomas.   2. Autism—Patients—United States—Biography.   3. Fields-Meyer, Ezra—Mental health.
4. Autistic youth—Biography.   5. Parents of autistic children.   I. Title.
  RC553.A88F53 2011
  616.85'8820092—dc23   2011014572
  [B]

Set in ITC Berkeley Old Style
Designed by Alissa Amell

Printed in the United States of America

PUBLISHER'S NOTE
Penguin is committed to publishing works of quality and integrity. In that spirit, we are proud to offer this book to our
readers; however the story, the experiences, and the words are the author's alone.
    While the author has made every effort to provide accurate telephone numbers and Internet addresses at the time of
publication, neither the publisher nor the author assumes any responsibility for errors, or for changes that occur after
publication. Further, publisher does not have any control over and does not assume any responsibility for author or third-
party Web sites or their content.

For my parents,
Lora and Jim Meyer,
who were always there,
following me

Blessed are You, Lord our God, Sovereign of the universe,
Who creates variety among living beings.

—Traditional Jewish blessing

CONTENTS

Contents

FOLLOWING EZRA

Following Ezra

The walk was always the same. Then one day it was different.

In the summer of 1999, my wife Shawn and I spent two months with our three young sons at a retreat center nestled in the arid foothills bordering Simi Valley, California. The campus was a spectacular, sprawling property stretching over gentle, golden ridges dotted with eucalyptus, pepper trees, and cactus. Shawn, a recently ordained rabbi, was teaching Jewish texts and practices to a group of young adults. The job required long hours not only in the classroom but also in intense, private discussions of spirituality during meals in the dining hall, on long strolls, and over snacks late into the night. At the same time she was nurturing the souls of a few dozen twenty-somethings, we were also busy caring for our boys: Ami, who was five; Ezra, three; and Noam, eighteen months.

Some months earlier, Ezra had begun displaying troubling behavior. He isolated himself from his preschool classmates to flip mechanically through picture books. At home, he spent inordinate periods absorbed in solitary, odd activities like lining up plastic dinosaurs and jungle animals in precise, symmetrical patterns across the back porch. His sensory system was clearly in disarray. That summer, he was so tortured by the cacophonous noises of the dining hall that he would cover his ears and run out the doors; at nearly every breakfast, lunch, and dinner we had to designate an adult to keep track of Ezra as he paced alone in small circles on the concrete patio or sought out insects among the boulders and agave plants on a nearby hillside.

Ezra seemed agitated even in his sleep, and when he rose at daybreak, it fell upon me to prevent him from waking the other boys or creating enough of a disturbance to rouse the staff members and families neighboring our small bungalow.

So Ezra and I began taking walks.

The air was cool and crisp at that early hour, the best time to roam the grounds, where peacocks wandered freely and geckos scampered across stone walls and asphalt patches. Ezra was drawn to animals of all kinds, so we wandered down a short dirt road to visit a compact stable that housed the center's small herd of horses, then continued up a knoll and into a modest pen, where Ezra could meander amid a few dozen chickens and, nearby, peek into a small aviary with parrots and a handful of pigeons. For a boy who spent most of the year in a Los Angeles neighborhood with all of the traffic, smog, and noise that came with it, this was heaven.

After a few days, Ezra had worked out a circuit that he insisted on following each morning: paying a visit to the livestock and birds, then continuing a stretch to a little barn, past the swimming pool and sports fields, and up the road to where he had discovered a playground area. There, years before, campers had created a cluster of toddler-size animals molded from plaster. Ezra would sit on each one, always in exactly the same order: the giraffe, the camel, the snail, the turtle. Then we wandered to the nearby swing set, where I pushed him for a few minutes until he was ready to hop off and stroll back to the cabin, just in time to find his mother and brothers beginning to stir.

One morning, instead of turning left to return to the cabin, Ezra turned right.

"Other way, Ez," I said. But he didn't hear—or chose not to listen. Instead of heading back toward the family, he walked with resolve up the paved road, toddling a few steps ahead of me. I followed closely behind him, calling to him, to no avail. Then I dropped back a few paces. It was a private road, and I knew that at that early hour no cars were likely to come by, not even the groundskeeper's rusty red pickup. So I let my young son walk as I faded ten feet, then fifteen, then twenty feet behind. I wondered whether he might become upset, realizing that I was not at his side. He didn't. Ezra followed the curving road amid the brush and eucalyptus, up a small hill, around a bend, and on for nearly half a mile. A three-year-old boy ambling up a rural road, more and more isolated from everything and everyone he knew, my son seemed completely on his own—confident and naive, bold and aloof, utterly alone.

I watched, feeling a combination of fear, bewilderment, and wonder. Fear for his safety; bewilderment at his seeming lack of awareness or connection; wonder at his resolve to follow his own path, to take the road he wanted, even if it was unknown.

This is the story of what happened in the ten years following that summer, a decade that has delineated a personal journey, beginning in darkness, winding through desperation, fascination, love, and, ultimately, a sense of awe for our unique, exceptional son. I started the quest trying my best to be a good dad and an enlightened consumer, searching out the right doctors, the best therapy, the most promising medicine, the breakthrough diet. In time I learned that what I had been looking for was the wrong thing. Like many parents, I saw my son's challenges as something to get past so that my family and I could get on with our lives. I eventually learned that this *is* life; this is what life is. It wasn't about finding the right expert for my child; it was about learning to be the right parent.

Ten years ago, I watched my solitary boy venture down an isolated road. For a decade, I have watched from an increasing distance as he takes a path all his own. In some senses, that has made his life richer and fuller. Yet Ezra's path is so singular that I have wondered what he is missing by walking alone, in his discrete universe. And then there is this question: As his father, what is my role? To run ahead of him and lead him in a safe direction? To walk by his side, holding his hand? To try to pull him back to familiar territory? Long ago, I made my choice: to follow Ezra and to watch, in awe and mystery, as my son makes his own unique way in the world.

CHAPTER ONE

He's Gone

"Sorry about the chairs," the teacher says.

It's parent conference day at the preschool. As Shawn and I arrive on a chilly December morning, Karen gestures toward a pair of blue, toddler-size seats across a Formica-covered table from where she sits scanning a manila folder. Why do they always make us cram our adult bodies into these tiny chairs? It seems to reflect the absurdity of conducting conferences at a preschool. These two-year-olds aren't taking algebra exams or memorizing the branches of government. What could a teacher possibly have to say? I want to be a good father, but I'm not convinced it's worth taking the morning off from work and driving six miles to hear how my children are interacting with their Play-Doh.

I decide it is important, though, more to check on the school than the children. After moving from New York to Los Angeles just a few months earlier, we enrolled Ami and Ezra at the neighborhood preschool without much research besides soliciting recommendations from a couple of friends. The conference will give us a chance to get to know the teachers and to introduce ourselves.

We're impressed with Ami's instructor, an upbeat woman who regales us with stories about how well our oldest son has adjusted to the new environment. Ami, at four, has quickly forged friendships with virtually every child, distinguished himself by routinely volunteering to set up the apple juice cups, and charmed instructors with his smile and manners. "In fifteen years teaching preschool," she says, "I have rarely had a child like this."

Warmed and cheered by an educator who obviously knows what she is talking about, my wife and I smile at each other as we make our way a few doors down the hall to Ezra's room. Karen is in her mid-thirties, with short blond hair, and a languid manner that might be calming to young children, but her halting speech immediately makes the conversation feel as awkward as the chairs. After an initial nervous smile as she welcomes us, she quickly becomes more somber, looking over her notes.

"Let's start with the positives," she says, not smiling. "Ezra has a lot of energy and"—she pauses—"he's a very loving child." Then a long, difficult silence. I'm waiting to hear the rest of the positives, but none come. Just this: "I do have some concerns."

On only a few occasions in life have I felt time slow down. At our wedding, the births of our children, the moment I pulled onto Fairfax Avenue at the wrong second and watched another Toyota minivan careen into mine—events that stretched out, seemingly out of time, existing in their own reality, apart from the ordinary pace of the universe. This conference is becoming one of those moments. I hear some of the words—*spacy, inflexible, autonomous*—and the phrases—*hard to get him to connect, not very responsive*. I catch one image: Before snack, when the children get in line to wash their hands, Karen says, reading from her handwritten notes, Ezra simply stands at the sink, motionless, seemingly not understanding what to do. I picture my little boy, lost in thought as water flows from the tap and his classmates press up behind him, eager to get to their Ritz crackers and apple slices.

As the teacher describes our middle son, I look up at Shawn. We both understand what Karen is talking about. In recent months, we have begun to notice quirky behavior ourselves. Ezra has been spending long hours alone engaged in strange, solitary routines. He lines up his toys in precise patterns in the backyard, then turns on a garden spigot, leaving it running as he watches the water form a small rivulet across the concrete. Then he drags a plastic laundry basket outside and folds a multicolored comforter into it, then climbs in himself, tucking his body into the quilt and lying in silence as he listens to the running water. He repeats this ritual day after day. Occasionally he has gone missing in the house for fifteen or twenty minutes and we frantically search every room, finally discovering him hiding, awake but motionless, under a mound of stuffed animals he has crammed into his younger brother's crib.

To us, he seems remote and a bit unusual, but we figure that's just Ezra. He acts and responds to almost everything differently than Ami, who was outgoing and friendly seemingly from the moment he emerged from Shawn's womb. Isn't that to be expected? Doesn't every child have a unique personality?

My initial response to Karen's description is to smile. *Yep, that sounds like Ezra, all right.* Shawn, too, breaks into a grin of recognition. Then she asks what Karen has been doing to help our son adapt. Karen pauses for a long time, at a loss, then, looking down, quietly answers: "I'm telling *you.*"

I don't know what any of it means—how unusual his behavior is, what our next step should be—but as the two of us slip out of the school and slowly walk down the street, I feel a sense of alarm and disquiet like none I have known.

That night, Shawn can't sleep. Of course, we have both recognized our son's odd habits, but hearing the description from Karen has been a shock. His behavior isn't just odd; it's problematic. Surrounded by the rambunctious, animated play of other two-year-olds, he chooses to be alone, seeming to notice only the picture books he is continually paging through.

"He has difficulty focusing on tasks such as hand washing and drying, feeding himself and fine-motor activities," Karen has written on the two-page report she handed us on our way out of the classroom. "He often chooses to be by himself rather than interacting with peers."

Shawn has long felt baffled by Ezra. She's a natural and nurturing mother, constantly singing to the children, lavishing the boys with hugs and kisses, and enthusiastically engaging them in play. But Ezra has become resistant to her hugs, and she has expressed frustration and sadness at how our two oldest children don't interact easily the way she saw other siblings play. Ami seeks out friends and playmates, but he has little to do with Ezra, who shows no apparent need or desire for companions. Sitting up in bed, tears running down her cheeks, Shawn takes out a pad of paper and writes the words: *"Who and what is my son Ezra?"*

She lists these qualities of our two-year-old boy:

- Sweet!
- Musical—remembers words and melodies

- Articulate
- Very attached to me
- Happy
- Strong willed and determined
- Very into routine

Then she writes another list, under the heading *"Ezra does not"*:

- Eat much or regularly
- Socialize much with other kids
- Always respond when called
- Sleep late
- Sit for long at dinner
- Like to remain clothed

Finally, she makes a third column: *"Ezra likes"*:

- Snuggling in blankets
- Snuggling with me
- Bathing, playing with toys in bath
- Playing in porta-crib with his animal friends
- Watching videos
- Playing outside with water
- Hearing books read
- Sitting alone and looking through books

I'm not sure why she is compiling this inventory of our son's traits. I suppose Shawn is trying to exert some control—to make sense of the chaos.

My wife is not timid. She is assertive, self-confident, and operates with assurance. But not now. When it comes to Ezra, she seems uncharacteristically adrift. Writing it down helps. Just articulating the collection of behaviors and characteristics that she has been noticing, sometimes passively, seems to ease her mind. But it is also painful. When she's finished writing, Shawn looks over the pad of paper, shakes her head, and wipes a tear away.

My own response—to the list and the situation—is different. Part of me still thinks our son is fine; he simply needs an instructor who understands him. One of Karen's observations was that the teachers had brought in a plastic toddler-scale table meant for water play, and filled its shallow basin instead with dry oatmeal. Ezra, she reported, kept trying to eat the oatmeal, even when his teachers repeatedly asked him to stop. Who is right, I wonder—the ones playing with oatmeal, or the one eating it?

I have been a journalist for years, and I am trained to use research as the way to solve problems. When I shop for a camera or a printer, I study *Consumer Reports*, bring it along to Best Buy, and purchase the best product on the list. That keeps things simple. Shawn has already obtained the phone number of a family therapist the school recommends. I figure that we'll consult this woman, gather her advice, follow it, using the right technique to get him engaged with other kids and his teachers, and solve the Ezra problem.

A few days later, in an ordinary office building on a busy street, we visit Ruth. She is an angular woman, with a no-nonsense, grandmotherly style. Though the seating is more comfortable than in Karen's classroom—Shawn and I share a plush maroon love seat—I still feel anxious, off balance.

Ruth begins by taking a case history.

"Tell me about your pregnancy with Ezra," she says with a slight smile.

It began when we were spending a year—the third of six years of Shawn's rabbinical studies—in Jerusalem. We were leasing a small walk-up apartment in a pale stone building on a quiet, one-block side street called Tel Chai—Hebrew for "hill of life."

For me, it was a year of changed plans. I arrived with vague notions of pursuing my work as a freelance journalist, writing newspaper and magazine features about Israel. Instead I mostly cared for Ami, who was just over three months old when we arrived. While Shawn studied Talmud and Jewish law, I maneuvered the black fold-up stroller through the city's labyrinthine streets and the narrow passageways of the open-air produce markets, simultaneously becoming intimately acquainted with the ancient city and my infant son as I changed diapers in bus shelters and cafés.

We knew we wanted more children—maybe three or four more—and by the time we moved the next July to New York—where Shawn would complete her rabbinic studies and I landed a job writing for a weekly magazine—Shawn was into her second trimester.

Before long, we met in Manhattan's east seventies for a late-morning appointment with an ultrasound technician.

"You need to tell me if you want to *know*—or not," the young woman said as she squeezed bluish goop onto Shawn's belly and pushed some buttons on the sonogram machine.

We had talked about whether we wanted to learn the gender. We did, each of us for a different reason, and neither of us because we wanted to know whether the nursery should be painted blue or pink. For Shawn it was about control: Pregnancy was so wrought with uncertainty that she wanted the comfort of knowing something for sure. For me it was the journalist's instinct: If there was vital information available, I wanted to have it.

As the woman traced Shawn's belly with the sonogram's wand, we looked at the small monitor, trying to make sense of the blurry shapes appearing on the tiny screen. "There's the spine . . . the kidneys. You can see the little heart beating," she said. To me it looked more like bad video from one of the Apollo missions.

"Everything looks good and healthy," she said. "What's your older child—boy or girl?"

"A boy," we said in unison.

"Looks like he's going to have a brother."

Shawn and I smiled at each other, half surprised, half amused. Two boys.

And then something happened I couldn't explain. I decided on our son's name. In that moment, I simply knew. As long as Shawn and I had been together, I had been the indecisive partner, the one who labored over even the simplest choices—restaurants, birthday gifts, which movie to rent— and then second-guessed myself; her style was to make snap decisions (usually wisely) and never look back. We had chosen Ami's name, for instance, after collaborating on a list of criteria and then consulting a stack of books. (His full name, Amiel, was a combination of the Hebrew words for "my people" and God.) But as soon as the technician wiped the goop off Shawn's belly and left us, I told my wife our fetus's name.

"I think he's going to be Ezra," I told her. Hebrew for "help." It was not a name we had discussed. But I knew that was it.

Shawn mulled it over. "You *think*?"

"I think," I said.

*   *   *

"Anything unusual about your delivery?" Ruth asks.

In fact, it was traumatic. Ami had been born by cesarean section, and this time the doctor assured Shawn there was a good chance for what they called a VBAC, a vaginal birth after cesarean. But on that cold and rainy January afternoon, as I listened in on the neighboring birthing rooms, it seemed that a dozen or so moms had arrived, panted, screamed, delivered, and bonded with newborns while we sat waiting for Ezra to emerge. Then Dr. Morrone spotted blood in Shawn's catheter and decided to wheel her down the hall for a cesarean. It was all seeming familiar, an echo of Ami's birth, until—just minutes into the procedure—I saw the doctor shake her head and abruptly say six sobering words: "This baby's not coming out yet."

Suddenly panicked, I tried to secure an explanation, but had to wait while the doctors and nurses quietly conferred and I attempted to catch a glimpse of the fetal monitor to try to ascertain what was amiss. I imagined the possibilities, trying to block out the worst scenarios. It was stunning how quickly our joyous morning had morphed into anxious moments of dread, breathtaking how fine the line was between celebration and crisis. Finally, Dr. Morrone turned to clue me in. Stepping away from Shawn and the other gowned medics for a moment, she lowered her voice and gave me an explanation: The scar tissue from Shawn's first C-section had caused her bladder to adhere to her uterus. That meant that instead of delivering the baby immediately and stitching Shawn back together in minutes, the surgeons needed to perform a long, difficult dissection.

"This could take some time," she told me.

"How long?" I asked.

"We'll do it as quickly as we can, but we need to be careful."

I stood in a corner of the room while the doctors worked on Shawn, who was wide-awake, under only local anesthesia. About an hour into the procedure, Ezra emerged with a thick head of jet-black hair and a healthy cry. Shawn held him briefly on her chest, but quickly the doctors—clearly concerned—handed the baby to me while they worked on my wife.

For the first half hour of his life, I held Ezra, who was tightly swaddled and silent, while I paced in the corner of the operating room in my scrubs, quietly singing to my newborn the only song that came to mind: "*Yerushalayim Shel Zahav*" ("Jerusalem of Gold"), a Hebrew song about the holy city where we had lived when the pregnancy began. All the while, I worried about my wife, who lay, arms extended on platforms—a young rabbinical student laid out like Jesus on the cross. A nurse put the baby in a bassinet and gently but firmly asked me to leave the operating room and accompany my son to the nursery. I asked how long the surgery would take. She shrugged, a puzzled look on her face.

Filled with a mix of joy over our new baby and deep concern for my wife, I spent the afternoon walking the hallways of Mount Sinai Hospital, shuttling between the nursery and the operating room, where I awaited word of Shawn's condition. Outside was a pounding rainstorm. At one point, I saw a man in a sopping trench coat rush from the elevator to the operating room. It turned out he was the urologist Dr. Morrone had called in to inspect Shawn's bladder and make sure it was undamaged before they stitched her back together.

Finally, after more than four hours of surgery, an orderly wheeled Shawn—spent and exhausted—from the OR to the recovery room. Down the hall, Ezra lay in the nursery, easily distinguished by a Sid

Vicious hairdo—spiky, jet-black hair that seemed to announce that our newborn wasn't going to be like any of those other kids.

Ruth continues throwing us questions: When did Ezra first eat solid foods? When did he cut his first tooth? How old was he when he said his first words? With Ami we had noted and celebrated each land-mark achievement, but with the bustle of two children and our busy lives, those milestones in Ezra's development are growing hazier in both of our minds. I wonder: Have we done something wrong?

"Does he have any birthmarks?" Ruth asks.

Just one that we can think of: a light brown patch on his upper back. *Birthmarks*, I think. *What do birthmarks have to do with anything?*

"When was the first time he cried when somebody besides the two of you held him?"

Neither of us can recall—not because of fuzzy memory, but because it has practically never happened. Ezra seemed to be such a well-adjusted baby that he had earned himself a nickname: "Easy Ez." In his first year, he was calm, independent, and rarely needed soothing. When we moved to Los Angeles and enrolled him at the preschool, he didn't exhibit any kind of anxiety, bounding into Karen's classroom on the first morning and never looking back, though he didn't know any of the children. The other moms and dads hugged their little ones good-bye, then—following the teacher's instructions—lingered in the hallway for the first few mornings, peering through the small square window to see how their boys and girls were faring. Occasionally, Karen summoned a parent to come back in and comfort a sobbing toddler. When she waved me off with a grin—"*You* can go; he's fine"—I felt proud of our little guy, maybe even a bit smug.

Now it seems that what appeared then to be his confidence and independence might have been a red flag. So is his preference for wrapping himself in blankets and hiding in his little brother Noam's crib.

As I listen to the litany of questions and ponder our answers, I am starting to register how very different Ezra is.

I remember the urgent call I received one afternoon at my office from Shawn—working part-time and home in the afternoons—who was barely consolable.

"I can't find Ezra!" she said. "I've looked everywhere."

"Did you try the backyard?" I asked.

"Everywhere!"

I told her to check the crib, his favorite spot. Of course, she already had. She hung up, then called back five minutes later.

"He's not here," she said. "I'm going to call nine-one-one."

Eight miles away, peering out my sixteenth-floor office window, I gazed at the condo high-rise across the street, surveyed the busy traffic on Wilshire Boulevard, and looked toward the distant Santa Monica Mountains. Feeling helpless and confused, I imagined our little boy wandering the streets, a distant gaze on his face, a stuffed animal or two under his arm. I tried to think where he might wander, how far he could roam in our leafy residential neighborhood, with its gently curving streets. I had noticed teenage drivers speeding down our street, oblivious that it was a place where families with children lived. I wondered if he would have the instinct to avoid walking off the curb and into—

Then the phone rang again. Shawn was weeping—this time because she had found him. Ezra had been hiding at the back of a shelf in a deep linen closet upstairs. He had gone to the effort of climbing up, crawling in, shutting the folding louvered door, and then sliding to the back, behind a pile of blankets and towels. Ecstatic to find him, Shawn had reached out her arms to embrace him. Ezra had crawled out, jumped down, and scooted away, as if he hadn't seen her.

"What's the *matter* with him?" Shawn pleaded into the phone. "I don't understand what I did *wrong!*"

She has the same question now, as we sit on the love seat across from Ruth. The tears are less intense, but after reviewing the catalog of observations about our idiosyncratic middle child to this relative stranger, Shawn finally tells Ruth what she is thinking.

"I keep wondering," she says, "how much of this is our fault."

The question hangs in the air. I think of how much adoring energy we lavished on Ami for the twenty months he was our only child. We simply aren't able to devote the same kind of focus to Ezra. I wonder whether our second son, forced to compete for attention with an older brother, has— consciously or not—responded by withdrawing.

"That, I can answer," Ruth says. I wait. "You had nothing to do with it. This is one hundred percent wiring."

Wiring. That word jolts my mind, leaving me feeling at once relieved and devastated. Here is a woman who has surely raised her own family, who is an authority on children, who has never met my son, but simply from hearing our description knows that something is amiss—with his *wiring.* When Shawn was pregnant, she did everything to follow her doctor's instructions, taking the prescribed folic acid supplements as a hedge against birth defects—as if tiny white tablets in an orange plastic vial could protect against forces unknown. What came to mind at the time, if I gave it any thought, were things like physical deformities or serious terminal illnesses, disorders with names I knew but little understood. I don't know what *wiring* means. It isn't our fault. Okay. But *wiring*—that doesn't sound like an issue we can resolve in a few appointments with Ruth. That sounds permanent. The word echoes in my mind.

Her diagnosis doesn't get much more specific than that. Even after she spends a morning observing Ezra in the classroom and then we bring him for a visit, Ruth doesn't give a name to whatever is causing his withdrawal. She explains that she doesn't see value in slapping a label on such a young child while his mind is still developing. Of course, by now, all of the possible answers have swirled through my mind. In 1998, autism is a relatively rare diagnosis, and to me it conjures up images of a child silently rocking in a corner, limbs flailing helplessly. That's not Ezra. Besides, despite what Ruth has said about wiring, she explains that what might appear to be permanent often turns out to be a stage that the child outgrows.

It might not be a disorder. It might be a phase.

Either way, she does have ideas about how to work with him.

"We're going to play with your son," Ruth says. "But we're not going to choose the game. We're going to let him decide, and we're going to follow his lead."

She explains the approach in its simplest form: If Ezra chooses a truck, then as he pushes the toy, one of us might put a hand out to block the truck. That will lead to an interaction. Then we'll build on that encounter, forcing him to confront the parent doing the blocking. The goal is not to disrupt his play or to cause him frustration, but to turn his isolated play into a social interaction, and then to build on that. In time, we will draw him away from his solitary, repetitive activities and into our lives.

Or at least that's the theory.

*   *   *

Every Wednesday, Shawn and I bring Ezra to Ruth's office, where
the four of us sit on the carpeted floor. She opens a large wooden cabinet
full of toys and games, Ezra chooses a toy, and we follow his lead. Often,
he doesn't even choose a toy. He climbs up on the back of the couch. We
pretend it's a boat. He rolls in a blanket on the floor. I lie down and try to
roll with him. Ruth sits a few feet away, coaching us as we play. He is
most attracted to her collection of stuffed animals and puppets.

One Wednesday he selects a toy farm—a set of plastic animals nested
into a shoe box–size barn. We pretend to talk, taking on the role of the
duck or the farmer, and trying to elicit a reaction from Ezra, who remains
aloof. Ruth demonstrates how using a high-pitched, excited voice can
attract his attention and draw him in. High affect, she calls it. It takes a
bit of shedding inhibitions. On occasion it works, but I find myself feeling
somewhat absurd as I sit on the carpet holding a tiny cow or goose
between my thumb and forefinger and making animal noises. Sometimes
keeping the conversation going feels like struggling to keep a sinking
boat afloat, or tapping a balloon to keep it aloft, only to watch it escape
your reach and slowly fall to the ground. But I trust Ruth's instinct that
all of this play will help our son to connect in ways that don't seem to
come naturally. I take it one week at a time, not yet perceiving this as
anything greater than a way to get our preschooler back on track. But
it's a struggle. When Ezra withdraws, Ruth indicates it with a short
pronouncement: "He's *gone*." And it feels that way: like he's departed,
transported himself to some other place. He seems far away.

One afternoon, Ezra doesn't want to play with any of the toys, and
keeps looking away from us. At first I think he is staring at the wall, but

then I realize he is keenly focusing on some object. On the large expanse of wall he has spotted a tiny spider, so the spider becomes the game. Shawn starts talking to the spider. I speak in the voice of the spider, then in a loud whisper tell Ezra to ask the spider where he is going.

"Where he's going?" he says, echoing my words.

"I'm trying to find my home," I say, then whisper to Ezra to ask if the spider has a web.

"If he has a web?" he echoes.

The three of us sit on the floor, watching together and trying to maintain the interaction as Ezra, mesmerized, keeps his eyes fixed on the spider crawling up the wall, onto the ceiling, and, finally, into a vent.

"All gone," Ezra says.

"All gone," we echo.

Increasingly, Ezra too seems all gone. At home, our son is falling into a solitary world of plastic animals, animated videos, and plush toys—a place Shawn has come to call "Planet Ezra."

He does not appear to be forming any friendships in Karen's class. The children are young enough that "parallel play" is typical, but Ezra still stands out for his lack of connection. Baffled about how to plan his third birthday party, Shawn invites the entire class and hires a young actress to entertain the kids with parachute games and balloon animals. But when the woman gathers the children in a circle in our living room and pulls out her guitar to begin singing, Ezra is . . . gone. I run upstairs and discover him alone in his bedroom, jumping up and down and talking to himself. As the sound of toddlers singing "She'll Be Coming 'Round the Mountain" wafts up the stairs, I watch my son pretending to be Tigger, whom he has watched over and over on a favorite video.

"Ezra, come on down. It's *your* party!" I plead.

"Hellooo! Hellooo!" he calls, not to me, but to nobody—to himself, or perhaps to the Winnie the Pooh in his head—as he keeps bouncing, seeming not to hear me. *"Hellooo!"*

It is difficult to know how to respond. This is the party we had planned for him, yet suddenly it seems entirely inappropriate for him. In fact, the whole life we had planned for him is seeming more and more inappropriate.

We discuss that one afternoon back at Ruth's office, as Shawn and I once again try sitting on the floor, making vain efforts to engage our son in play. Shawn in particular is finding the experience increasingly frustrating. The harder we try to engage him, the more Ezra resists, and the more isolated he becomes. He isn't defiant, just detached—his voice distant, his gaze diffuse. Elsewhere, Shawn is a dynamic, confident, upbeat woman, full of life and energy. She is also a master communicator, able to command a room as a teacher of rabbinical students and at the small congregation she leads, where she engages adult learners in lively, interactive spiritual discussions. She pours herself into deep conversations with her circle of women friends and with me. Yet here, for the hour we focus on Ezra, she is often discouraged and bewildered at this growing realization: She cannot communicate with her own son.

One afternoon on the maroon love seat, I hold Shawn's hand, silently listening to my wife, exasperated, wonder tearfully how she will ever get through to Ezra.

Ruth listens and nods with understanding.

"You have to allow yourself to grieve," she says.

I speak up: "For what?"

"You have to let yourself grieve for the child he didn't turn out to be."

I let that echo in my mind.

Grieve for the child he didn't turn out to be.

I have not spent much time with therapists. I was lucky enough to grow up in relative happiness. My parents' marriage was strong. My family of five (like Ezra, I was the second of three sons) has always been close and nurturing. I excelled in high school and went to a good college. The toughest moments of my life were minor rites of passage: the deaths of my grandparents, and occasional girlfriend problems. I went from college to a successful career as a writer for newspapers and national magazines. At the right time I ran into Shawn, an old childhood friend, and we fell in love and into a strong, supportive marriage. None of that has prepared me for this.

Grieve for the child he didn't turn out to be.

That night, I'm the one who can't sleep. Not because of Ezra. Because of Ruth. As I lie awake, I keep hearing her voice, her quiet tone, her calm delivery.

Grieve for the child he didn't turn out to be.

And I realize something: I am not grieving. In fact, I feel no instinct to grieve. When I thought about becoming a father, when Shawn and I dreamed together and planned together and decided to start raising a family, I carried no particular notion of who our children would become. I have seen plenty of my friends over the years damaged by their own parents' expectations and disappointments—that a girl wasn't a boy; that a younger child didn't measure up to an older one; that a child didn't want to be a doctor after all. Perhaps because of that, or perhaps because of some glitch in my own wiring, I didn't carry any conscious notion of what my children would be like—whether they would be girls or boys, tall or short, conventional or a little bit odd.

I planned only to love them.

The next week, when we visit Ruth, I tell her that.

"I don't feel that way," I say. "I'm not going to grieve."

I am sure she thinks that I am deluding myself. I know the truth. That one statement has done more good for me than all of the play therapy, than all of the listening, all of the advice. It has forced me to find and bring out something within myself. I feel full of love—for the boy who lines up the dinosaurs on the porch, for the child pretending to be Tigger in his bedroom, for the little one I carried and sang to in the first minutes of his life. My answer will never be to mourn. It will be to pour love on my son, to celebrate him, to understand, to support him, and to follow his lead.

CHAPTER TWO

A Different Mind

One evening, I try to put Ezra to bed one hundred times in a row. And that is just the beginning.

The trouble is, I'm following instructions that were written for another kid.

Every generation of parents has its bible. Like many new mothers and fathers of the nineties, Shawn and I have learned much of what we know about raising young children from a series of books called *What to Expect*. Throughout her first pregnancy, Shawn kept a copy of *What to Expect When You're Expecting* on her nightstand next to the volumes of the Talmud and Torah commentaries she was studying in rabbinical school. When Ami, our firstborn, was a few weeks old, we followed *What to Expect the First Year*'s precise, step-by-step instructions for bathing an infant as if they were Julia Child's directions for preparing the perfect soufflé. ("Have all of the following ready before undressing baby . . ." and "Slip baby gradually into the bath, talking in soothing and reassuring tones to minimize fear, and holding on securely to prevent a startle reflex. . . .")

We once learned at the feet of the book's mastermind, a sweet and grounded grandmother named Arlene Eisenberg who taught parenting workshops in the Manhattan neighborhood where we lived before moving to Los Angeles. Peppered with questions about potty training and vitamins, she repeated like a mantra a phrase she said applied equally to toddlers and teens: "Love and limits." She urged that if we later recalled nothing else she said that night, we remember those words: *love and limits.*

We never forgot.

What neither Arlene nor her *What to Expect* books have explained to us is what you are supposed to do when *nothing* is what anyone expected. Ezra, like Ami before him, developed in pace with the milestones in the parenting books for the first eighteen months, but then things veered off course. The book doesn't say what to do when your child spends long hours in a foggy trance, or when he answers every question by repeating a few words of the question, looking off into space:

ME: "Ezra, do you want a banana or an apple?"
EZRA: "Ezra, you want a banana?"
ME: "Tell me which one you want."
EZRA: "Tell me which one."

The book's index doesn't point readers to any ready-made instructions to follow when your child shows no whiff of interest in other boys and girls. And no matter how much love we offer and how many limits we try to impose, we cannot break Ezra's habit of routinely rummaging through the shelves of the playroom and dumping the contents of every bin, every box, every puzzle onto the floor, creating huge, chaotic mounds of LEGOs, Slinkys, wooden blocks, and game pieces.

Still, when we run into trouble, my instinct is always to seek out instructions and follow them. A relative novice at child rearing, I trust that others who have been through it can tell me how. That is the attitude I bring to the challenge of getting Ezra to sleep.

In our division of labor, bedtime has fallen into my parenting portfolio, while Shawn handles playdates, babysitters, birthday cakes, and much of the snuggling. Maybe it happened when Ami, our eldest, was a toddler. Shawn was a graduate student and I worked at the magazine by day, usually returning home in the evening at precisely the time my wife needed to focus on homework and Ami needed to get to bed. Or, more likely, I took it on because I saw it as a problem that I could solve—if only I was able to do the right research and consult the right experts.

When Ami went through the transition from crib to bed, Shawn and I sought advice from our pediatrician and consulted with friends and coworkers and relatives. On the subway to work, I studied from a stack of books with names like *Winning Bedtime Battles* and *Solve Your Child's Sleep Problems*. Eventually, we devised a hybrid system, a mix of love and limits that involved a bath, a comforting bedtime story, and a sweet lullaby— followed by a door held tightly closed from the outside (the most popular book's suggestion) until Ami bawled himself into exhaustion. That led to many months of frustration, second-guessing, late-night cuddling, pleading, and fine-tuning, until eventually Ami simply took matters into his own hands and taught himself to go to bed.

The house we are renting in Los Angeles has three children's bedrooms upstairs, but our sons are accustomed to sharing space from our time in a small New York apartment. For the first few months, Ami and Ezra share a room, but then Ezra, three years old, starts becoming so agitated at bedtime that his noise and movement are keeping Ami awake. So we move Ezra down the hall into his own room.

That brings a whole new chapter of sleep issues, and I am determined to avoid the months of struggle we once endured with Ami. Instead of consulting the stack of books, I adopt one snippet of common sense I come across in an earthy, no-nonsense guidebook called *The Mother's Almanac*. Its essential wisdom: Follow a comforting bedtime routine—a story, a song, and a good-night kiss. If the child gets out of bed, simply tuck him back in, "not angrily, but a little more businesslike every time." The key: no drama. The first night or two, it might take an hour but, offers the book, "By the end of the first week, the problem is almost always over, no matter how old the child."

The first night in his new room, Shawn reads Ezra a book, we sing him a lullaby together, we tuck him in, we both kiss him good night, I switch off the light, and we leave, slipping into our bedroom across the hall.

Easy.

Two minutes later, I look up to see Ezra at our door, his almond-shaped brown eyes looking at me behind his straight dark brown bangs. Without a word, I pick him up and walk him back, tucking him in again.

"Good night," I say calmly.

Two minutes later, he returns. Again, I walk him back.

"Good night."

Again, Ezra emerges. I return him, then quietly sit on the floor in the hall, thinking about the book: *The first night or two, it might take an hour. . . .*

He's back. I deposit him on his bed again: "Good night." No drama. I repeat the process, more businesslike each time. And each time, Ezra bounces to his feet.

The book was right. The first time, it takes an hour to get Ezra to sleep. The second night, though, he's still awake and alert after *two* hours—more than one hundred repetitions of the cycle. Determined, disciplined, and confident in the wisdom of the authors, I stick with the plan, keeping in mind their assurance: *By the end of the first week, the problem is almost always over.*

The third night I post myself on a chair just outside Ezra's door, eager to see the system begin to work. But that night it takes even *longer*. For more than two hours I'm walking back and forth on the stretch of carpet from my chair to his bed. I'm still trying to be businesslike—zombielike is more like it—but I am beginning to question the plan I have chosen to follow. By the fourth evening, Ezra seems excited for bedtime, and I feel hopeful that this might be the night when the system kicks in.

No such luck. The more frequently I scoop up my three-year-old and drop him back into bed, the more awake he seems. *The problem is almost always over*, the book promises. I start reading the passage like a lawyer, noticing the word I had glanced over before: *almost*. It has been four days, and my problem isn't *nearly* over. My problem is *worse*. When I repeatedly return Ezra to his bed, I'm not soothing him into drowsiness. He's being *stimulated*. What was supposed to get him to sleep is, instead, waking him up. The repetition that would knock out almost any other child is, to him, a tantalizing tonic he has come to crave like a crack addict seeking his fix.

In that moment, sitting wearily in the hallway outside his room, I come to realize something: Ezra has a different kind of mind. The rules that make sense with other children simply don't work with him. The predictable, orderly world of *What to Expect* and the growing collection of other parenting books on our shelves doesn't exist for him. The wisdom we have drawn on to raise our first child so far isn't going to be effective with this one. All bets are off. We're on our own.

It's not just his mind that is different. By age four, Ezra seems uncomfortable in his clothing, stripping off his shirt and pants as soon as he walks into the house—and often in the homes of other people, even when he doesn't know them well. A couple we've met in the neighborhood invites us for a weekend lunch, and—friendly and nonjudgmental as they're trying to be—seem hard-pressed to act nonchalant when Ezra squirms out of his booster seat within minutes, removes every piece of clothing, and then starts running laps around the table.

His instincts seem to be the opposite of what any other child might feel. At the playground of a nearby park, he rides the merry-go-round at full speed, imploring, "Faster! Faster!" no matter how fast it is spinning, and then walks off in a straight line, his steps and posture steadier and surer than before. On the swing set, he begs, "Higher! Higher!" even when the swing is already flying precariously above my head.

He craves the feeling of being tightly squeezed, pleading for Shawn and me to roll him up in a blanket, and then demanding that we do it again, only more snugly. He climbs under heavy objects—mattresses, area rugs—but flees from his mother's embrace and shakes his body away to avoid holding my hand. On sultry days he nestles into heavy comforters. At the pizza parlor he demands a single regular slice, cut in half—he calls it "broken plain" (which we misinterpret initially as having something to do with a disabled aircraft). He won't eat it before touching the surface with an index finger to make sure the pizza is so hot that it seems sure to scald his mouth. He refuses to consume a banana if it is not whole, and secretly sneaks whole bricks of cheddar cheese from the fridge, gnawing at them like a rodent. He is drawn to feeling the textures of all kinds of fabric, obsessively pulling fibers out of quilts or clothing and chewing on them, sometimes purposely ingesting the threads.

He has a compulsion to test unknown textures with his tongue, occasionally fingering the carpeting in a doctor's office lobby or an unfamiliar house and then, intrigued, getting on all fours and licking. We try to stop him, but he appears to be almost magnetically attracted, unable to pull his body away. Once, while visiting a neighbor's house, I notice black fragments of something on Ezra's hands and teeth and ask where it came from. He won't say, so I snoop around in the backyard, where Ezra has been exploring. There, I follow a trail of the black bits leading to the large air-conditioning unit and assemble the story in my mind: Apparently curious about the look and the feel of the black foam insulation around a duct from the unit, he has peeled some away and tried to chew on it. Almost daily, he unzips the sofa cushions, pulls out wads of fluffy synthetic stuffing, and spreads it across the floor, calling it snow or cotton candy. It's not enough to scold him about this. He seems incapable of stopping himself.

He defies gravity. From the time he was two, Ezra has seemed driven to climb almost anything, as if he's trying to escape the bounds of earth. That compulsion is combined with a fearlessness that I find both extraordinary and alarming. Once, on a visit to relatives in Connecticut, as our family of five posed for photos on their front porch, Ezra slipped out of the frame and scaled a nearby garden trellis, not stopping until he was well above us, dangerously out of reach. At our dinner table, he climbs on Shawn's body, clambering from her lap onto her shoulders, and occasionally sitting atop her head as she tries to eat. At a neighborhood park, as little girls hold a pretend tea party in a miniature pergola, Ezra scales the side of the structure, climbs onto the metal mesh canopy, and balances precariously there, oblivious to the children below. Nannies and moms flash looks of concern that say, *Who in God's name would let their kid do that?*

Me.

The climbing finally catches up with Ezra one winter morning when he is four. Shawn and I are awakened before dawn by a crash, and then the sound of someone screaming. I run out to the playroom and find Ezra running toward us in nothing but underwear.

"I broke myself! I broke myself!" he is screaming as he sobs. "I fell down! I broke myself!"

The playroom is in disarray, with stuffed animals and plastic bins strewn about—no different from most other times. I examine him for damage, and it takes a few moments to find the wound, a deep, bleeding puncture on the left side of his lower abdomen. It looks as if he has been stabbed. My first thought is that Ezra has punctured a lung. I look at his mouth, expecting him to start coughing up blood. He doesn't, but he is in distress.

"I broke my chest!" he keeps screaming. "Fix me, Abba!* Fix me!"

"What happened?" I ask. He can't tell me. While Shawn gathers some clothes for me, I grab my wallet and keys and look around the house. In the kitchen, I spot a chair out of place and, beside it, a door on a lower cabinet at an awkward angle, snapped from its upper hinge, wood splinters protruding. I piece together what happened. The previous night, I had stashed a box of cookies on the top shelf of a cabinet. Ezra had obviously seen me, so when he woke up to a quiet house, he decided to help himself. He climbed from the chair, planning to use the open lower

---

* Our children call us Abba and Ima, Hebrew terms for Dad and Mom.

cabinet door as a step stool, but when he stood on it, the hinge cracked, and as Ezra fell, the corner of the door jabbed his gut.

"Fever?" the orderly behind the desk at the emergency room says when he sees me rush in clutching my whimpering son. I shake my head and show him the wound. "He'll need stitches," the man says. The wait is nearly forty-five minutes. Ezra, in shock, clings to my body, moaning softly and occasionally nodding off. Shawn arrives—she has delivered the other boys to neighbors—and finally a nurse calls Ezra's name.

"We'll have to hold him down," the ER doctor tells us. A nurse wraps Ezra in a sheet to control his arms. I grasp his shoulder. The nurse steadies his head. It takes just a few minutes for the doctor to apply sutures; it's a remarkably quick procedure, especially considering my early fears upon finding Ezra that morning. As soon as the doctor tells my son he is finished, Ezra hops onto his feet, ready to leave, completely—almost eerily—back to normal.

"*Good-bye*, Nurse!" he says. "Thank you!"

As we walk to the car, I hold on to his arm and wonder whether the experience might teach him to be more cautious. I doubt it. When it comes to his body, Ezra seems incapable of using logic to control impulses. No matter how many times we warn him to be careful, he seems drawn to the climbing, the swinging, the spinning in ways that defy normal bounds.

We learn later that therapists have their own way of saying that: he lacks normal proprioception, the body's sense of where it is in space in relation to other objects and people. He doesn't know where his body is—unless he is wrapped tightly, or feeling intense physical pressure, or—best of all—in water. When Ezra is in the bathtub, surrounded by his toys, he becomes exceptionally calm and quiet. When we visit friends who have a Jacuzzi tub in their backyard, he settles in for hours, magnetically drawn to the womblike feeling and rhythm. In swimming pools, his entire body enveloped in warm water, he magically transforms into a chattier, more connected version of himself—and experiences a serenity that lasts for an hour or longer.

Just as he seems comforted, so are Shawn and I, discovering that there are ways to bring Ezra some peace. Of course, much as he would like to, Ezra can't live in a hot tub. And it is difficult to escape what I am coming to understand is one of his foremost challenges: Our son is not comfortable in his own body.

Ordinary experiences unexpectedly cause him such extreme discomfort that they torture him. The summer he is three—the same one we spend at the retreat center in Simi Valley—his unkempt brown hair has started to bother us enough that I take Ezra into town for a haircut, randomly choosing the first salon I come across, in a strip shopping mall. Ezra expresses some resistance—but, I think, so do most kids at his age when it's time for a haircut. An expressionless hairstylist gestures for him to come to her chair. He climbs in, but then his body goes limp as he slides out of the seat and onto the floor. I lift him back in, and he slips out again. Finally, I sit on the chair myself, holding Ezra in my lap, and tell her she can start.

As soon as she lifts a comb to his head, Ezra screams.

"*Noooo!* Don't touch my hair!"

I reassure him: "She's just going to give you a haircut, sweetheart. She won't hurt you."

That doesn't help. But she tries again.

"*Nooooo!*" he screams.

Surely the woman has experienced fussy children, so she reassures him and simply starts cutting. Ezra shrieks. She keeps going, trying to calm him. By then, Ezra's crying and shouting are enough commotion for other patrons to notice. The manager approaches, holding some candy.

"It's okay, honey—it's just a haircut," she says, smiling and handing him a red lollipop. Ezra grabs it and throws it back in her face. This is not going as I planned. I'm wondering whether I should have researched hair salons a bit more carefully.

"Ezra!" I say firmly. "Say you're sorry."

He can't even hear me. The hairstylist, seemingly motivated by the challenge, continues hacking at his hair, and Ezra keeps squirming. When he can't get far enough away, he grabs the scissors out of her hand and hurls them to the floor. She steps back. She has seen crying kids before, but this might be a first.

"That's it!" I say, scooping my son up with me and helping him out of the smock. Ezra, with a bad half haircut and loose, cut hairs sprinkled across his face and neck, sprints toward the exit as the two women stand by, expressions of repugnance and disbelief crossing their faces. I grab his hand, mutter an apology, pay the bill and throw in a ten-dollar tip (I don't wait for the change; I just want to escape), and chase my son out into the sizzling August afternoon.

Driving away, I look at Ezra in the rearview mirror, his eyes red and puffy from the crying, his brown hair trimmed in some places, still scruffy in others. As the motion of the car helps to calm him down, I ponder what could explain how an ordinary haircut escalated into a violent standoff. I once understood that having children meant sacrificing some sense of control, but more and more I find myself in situations like the one at the hair salon that seem completely out of hand, and beyond my ability to manage.

That night, Shawn and I wait until Ezra is finally asleep, and then she pulls out a pair of office scissors and a comb to try finishing the job Ezra had put a stop to at the salon. For many months after that, we let his hair grow long and unkempt. When it gets out of hand, we sneak up on him in his sleep, and Shawn does her best to trim the fine brown strands falling across his forehead without waking him up. Occasionally, she tries coaxing him to balance on the pedestal sink in our bathroom with a towel under him to catch the hair, but he can endure that for only a minute or two. That's what serves as a haircut.

Until we discover Hugh, the special-needs barber.

It has been nearly a year and a half since Ezra's disastrous encounter at the salon. Shawn asks around, and a woman at Ezra's school produces a scrap of paper with a handwritten name, Hugh, and a phone number. It turns out the salon is in Pacific Palisades, an upscale community more than half an hour's drive from our home. There are probably a few hundred hair salons and barbershops spread across West Los Angeles between our home and the Palisades, including a handful specifically for children. But we're desperate and figure it's worth a try. She makes an appointment, and I pick up Ezra at school on a rainy Thursday afternoon. To sweeten the deal, Shawn has told Ezra that he will be getting a new video, so we stop to pick one up, then find our way to a small, two-story shopping center not far from where Sunset Boulevard ends at the Pacific.

Hugh is a stout, balding man in his late thirties in a T-shirt and jeans. He works alone in a salon that's simple and sparse: a barber chair upholstered in deep red vinyl, a table, one mirror, a magazine rack, a small TV, and a green plastic patio chair. Hugh is finishing another boy's haircut when we walk in, so Ezra sits on the floor, where he is overjoyed to discover a large green bin full of plastic dinosaurs, just like his collection at home. He begins rifling through the dinosaurs until Hugh finishes with the other boy and pats the vinyl chair, indicating for Ezra to sit down.

I vaguely explain the hairstyle we're looking for. What I don't say is that, really, anything decent will be fine. Ezra's hair has been so unevenly cut for so long that it will be a relief to have a trim, period.

"Sure, surfer cut," Hugh says. He takes out a can of talcum powder and shows it to Ezra, letting him feel it on his fingers.

"Now, my friend, I'm going to put some of this on your neck, so it's not so itchy," he explains tenderly.

Before each step in the process, he offers Ezra a warning.

"My friend, I'm going to comb your hair now. That okay?" Before he sprays my son's hair with water, he grabs Ezra's hand and sprays gently into his palm.

"Don't cut my ear off!" Ezra says at one point, ducking to avoid the scissors. "You're going to cut my *ear* off!"

Hugh calmly takes Ezra's little hand in his, and shows Ezra how to hold his own ear flap down to keep it out of harm's way. When Ezra moans or cries, he asks, "Can you use your words, my friend?" Each time he speaks to Ezra, he uses that same phrase: *my friend*.

Even with all of that help, Ezra gets antsy, slouching to avoid Hugh's comb and scissors, and eventually letting his body slide out of Hugh's reach and onto the floor. I have been here before; I'm starting to feel like I'm back at the last salon, the site of the Great Haircut Disaster.

"Come on, Ezra!" I say. "Sit up! Let Hugh finish."

But Hugh waves me off. "Give him a minute. He just needs a break."

From the looks of it, Hugh is running behind schedule. His next two clients are already here, a girl sitting in the green plastic chair and a boy playing a video game in the corner. Now on the floor, Ezra scoots over to the bucket of dinosaurs, and starts reaching for them.

"Ezra! It's not time for that!" I say. "Come on!"

Hugh waits patiently. "He'll be up," he says calmly. "He just needs a second."

Ezra begins lining up the dinosaurs in a pattern, just as he likes to do at home, one creature at a time: tyrannosaurus, stegosaurus, triceratops. I look anxiously at my watch, peer at the waiting customers, and glance at Hugh. "It's okay," he says, nearly closing his eyes as he stands—unhurried, serene—with one hand on the back of the chair.

In a minute, Ezra has placed the last dinosaur. Without prompting, he stands upright and hops up in the chair. "Okay," he says steadily. "Ready."

Hugh keeps going. He has a magical, intuitive touch. I ask how he came to work with children like Ezra. Hugh has been cutting hair in children's salons since high school. Whenever a child who seemed problematic or difficult came in, "everyone else would freak out," he says, "and I would say, 'Come on. What's the big deal?'" He tells me that his colleagues had been afraid of what might happen, afraid of people different from themselves. "People don't give children enough credit," he says. "They're *people*."

By this point in the conversation, Ezra has slipped off the chair again, this time to explore the video game in the corner (the other boy has finished), a driving game with a steering wheel. Undeterred, Hugh trails him with his scissors, taking a minute to show Ezra how the game works, and then, as Ezra takes the wheel, putting the finishing touches on the back of his neck. As I watch the two of them, I feel grateful, even buoyant. In all of our searching for expert advice, for instructions to follow, I have discovered wisdom and insight in the most unlikely place—a children's hair salon near the beach. Even if our lives have veered off the course of *What to Expect*, there is hope, there are answers, and if we know where to look, we just might find angels along the way.

CHAPTER THREE

Lots of Little Fears

Everyone is afraid of something: precarious heights, closed places, darkness, sharks. Ezra is afraid of many things, and he seems to accumulate new fears the way other people collect stamps or seashells. Certain toys, unexpected noises, particular moments in animated videos—any of these can instill dread and dismay, usually without warning.

It happens at the Regional Center, the agency that distributes state dollars for children with various conditions that are classified as developmental disorders: cerebral palsy, Down syndrome, and autism, among others. When Ezra is just over three, Shawn and I learn that we need to find a way to get Ezra into the Regional Center system in order to obtain services for him. I keep hearing that word: *services*. I'm not certain what it means, or why Ezra needs them. I don't cope well with bureaucracies and lack the patience for paperwork. (I would never think of preparing my own tax return, instead handing my accountant an unruly heap of manila folders each spring.) But I know we need services—whatever that means—so we make contact.

A social worker named Denise visits the house on a sort of reconnaissance mission, a session to ascertain whether Ezra will meet the Regional Center's criteria. Denise is in her late forties, with a friendly manner. She sits with Shawn and me in the playroom—we've straightened up a bit, but there's no escaping the clutter of three children's oversize Lego blocks and plush toys—and she runs down a list of questions about Ezra. They're not much different from those we answered for Ruth—pregnancy, birth, first words—so we are prepared. I am also keenly aware of the strange, counterintuitive calculus at play. My instinct is to try to see our children in the best possible light, to find hope and filter out the more ominous indicators. Our goal in this transaction, though, isn't to make Ezra shine; Shawn and I need to make Denise understand that our son is troubled and challenged—that he is the kind of child who needs *services*.

We don't distort the truth. We tell Denise about the solitary play and the lack of connection. We describe how Ezra won't make eye contact, the way he repeats phrases, echoes questions, and often seems not to hear us at all.

"I think it's a good idea for you to bring him to meet one of our psychologists," Denise says when she's finished. I feel an odd mix of satisfaction and heartbreak. I close the door behind her and my wife and I share a warped moment of pride in our accomplishment: We have succeeded in presenting our son as troubled enough to qualify for the next round in the process.

A couple of weeks later, the three of us visit a large, bland office building in a business park in Culver City, about six miles from home. We're running late, and Ezra doesn't help when he presses every button he can reach on the elevator. The man in the suit heading for the top floor heaves a heavy sigh.

The second we step into Dr. Miller's office, Ezra gets a panicked look in his eyes and tries to turn around and head back for the door.

"What's wrong, honey?" says Dr. Miller—a petite woman with large eyeglasses and a warm smile.

Barely looking up, and shielding his eyes with his right forearm, he gestures with his left hand toward the corner behind her desk.

"I don't like that," he says.

We all look to see what he's pointing at. It's a puppet, a likeness of a character from a 1980s sitcom.

"Oh, Alf?" Dr. Miller says. "He's not scary; he's nice—look." She starts to mount the puppet on her right hand. Dr. Miller has a friendly, open manner and the kind of gentle, goofy enthusiasm children love in kindergarten teachers.

It doesn't help. Ezra looks terrified, holding both palms out in front of his face like he's fending off attackers. He shakes his head and looks downward, as if Alf's gaze will harm him.

"*Nooooo!*" he cries. "Make that go *away*."

She complies, stowing the creature in a metal file drawer.

"Okay?" Dr. Miller asks.

Ezra looks toward the drawer warily, as if he suspects that Alf could crawl back out at any moment and spray the room with gunfire.

"I'll even lock the drawer," she says, showing Ezra her key chain. "See?"

That helps, but Ezra is clearly still focused on Alf. His brown eyes dart about the office, scanning the shelves and surfaces for the next threat.

"That actually happens a lot," Shawn says to the doctor in a not-so-hushed whisper. "Lots of little fears."

Dr. Miller nods, trying to distract Ezra.

"Come with me," she says, gesturing to a small table.

For the next twenty minutes, she engages Ezra in a succession of tests: He draws shapes; he stacks wooden blocks; she shows him a series of pictures and asks him to explain what is happening in the sequence. Ezra mostly repeats the questions, or fragments of them—"What do you see?" "What are they doing?" He won't sit long at the table, instead wandering around the office, his back to the doctor as she speaks to him.

I don't understand most of the tests, and can't discern what would constitute success or failure, so it's difficult to know how to react or feel as I watch. I experience a tangle of emotions: Half of me is desperately rooting for Ezra, as if my kid's in a soccer game and I'm cheering from the bleachers. The other half deeply wants Ezra to fail. As I sit on a couch with Shawn, observing the process, I follow Dr. Miller's eyes, wondering whether she will recognize the same things we have been witnessing for weeks and months at home. I want her to confirm my own feelings and fears. And, of course, I want *services*.

In the midst of it all comes yet another flash of Ezra's irrational fear. Dr. Miller is leading us out of her office and down a corridor to visit one of her colleagues. Suddenly, without warning, Ezra starts and backs up, as if a wild beast has just dropped in his path.

"What is it, sweetheart?" Shawn asks.

He covers his ears with his hands—almost his whole arms—and hurries up the hall.

"Did something scare you?" she asks.

He hesitates, then finally answers.

"That," he says, pointing.

I look up. All I see is a drinking fountain mounted on the wall. I survey the expanse of the hallway to see if there's something I missed.

"The fountain?" Shawn asks. "You're scared of the drinking fountain?" The three of us stand there a moment with him.

"It's okay, Ezzy," Shawn says. "It's just a water fountain."

He keeps his palms on his ears, looking warily at the bubbler. I plant my hands on my thighs and lean forward, drawing my face close to his.

"Ez," I say, "what is it?"

"It made a noise," he says quietly.

"The fountain?"

He nods, then follows Dr. Miller and Shawn down the hall. A few paces up, he cranes his neck to glare at the fountain, as if he expects it to sprout legs and chase after him. Standing there a moment, I listen carefully. In a few seconds I hear the drinking fountain make a noise—the gentle hum of its electric motor. That's the sound that caused my three-year-old to jump in terror: *whrrrrrrrr*.

At least, I think, Dr. Miller saw what we wanted her to see.

A few minutes later, we're back in her office, where Shawn and I settle into the couch and she sits opposite us while Ezra plays alone on the floor.

"So, let's talk," she says. And then this: "I do think Ezra is on the autism spectrum."

It is the first time that we hear a professional give us the diagnosis for our son, who is just over three. In years to come I will listen to many parents who describe the moment they heard those words, or words like them, and how devastated they felt. Some will compare it to a punch in the stomach. Some will say they felt like they'd had all of the air sucked out of them. They describe disbelief, denial, shock. A blow like death itself.

I don't feel any of those things. The words hit me less as a dramatic revelation than as a step in a bureaucratic process. By the time we hear the word *autism* applied to our son, it feels almost like good news—like we've won some very twisted form of the lottery. It means we'll get services—which Dr. Miller explains could include a variety of therapies, enrichment programs, or help from caretakers to give us short respites from Ezra's care.

But before we get there, we ask her to explain.

"Autism doesn't describe a child," she says. "It describes a set of symptoms." No two children manifest it in the same way, she says, but Ezra has many of the characteristics: the echoing of words and phrases, known as echolalia; the repetition of words and sounds and motions, called perseveration; the lack of eye contact; the oversensitivity to sensory input—like bright lights or loud sounds, or even the sound of a drinking fountain's motor.

I ask her for an explanation. What accounts for this odd set of behaviors? She explains it not in terms of neurology or psychology, but with an analogy.

"Imagine that everything we experience is part of a movie," she says. "In order to see the movie, you need to run it through a projector. You and I have a projector, so we can put those frames together and watch the movie."

I nod, listening.

"Ezra can't see that movie. He's just got a hodgepodge of individual frames. When he tries to run it through the projector, it doesn't work. It's all fragmented. He can see an image here, an image there. But he can't put it all together and make sense of it all."

I find the analogy at once helpful and disturbing. It gives me a rough understanding of what is troubling my son, and why he seems to experience a fragmented, distracted reality.

"Our job now," she says, "is to give him the tools to put them together and make sense of the movie—or learn to live with them the way they are."

She gives us a few ideas for how to start: making schedule books with visual cues about what's going to happen every day, to ease the sense of anxiety that seems to grip Ezra at practically every moment; occupational therapy to help tame the sensory issues; and, she says, the most important ingredient, finding a preschool where he will fit in and where the educators know how to help. Shawn takes notes and I pretend to listen. In my mind, I'm stuck on Dr. Miller's image of my son desperately trying to make sense of a cluttered heap of movie frames. I'm lost trying to grasp Ezra's fractured consciousness.

On the way out, Ezra steers clear of the drinking fountain, and I think about how he lives with the new fears that arise around every corner, and wonder how I am going to live with mine.

If you have cancer, it shows up in a biopsy or an MRI scan. Doctors diagnose diabetes by measuring glucose levels in blood and urine. Diagnosing autism, it turns out, is an inexact science. In the absence of a blood test or a known genetic marker, professionals rely on a kind of Chinese food menu approach. The *Diagnostic and Statistical Manual of Mental Disorders, Fourth Edition*—known popularly as the *DSM IV*—begins its description of section 299.0, Autistic Disorder, by listing three categories: social interaction, communication, and restrictive and repetitive behavior. Each of the three categories includes a list of specific symptoms—things like "failure to develop peer relationships appropriate for social level," and "lack of varied, spontaneous and make-believe play . . ." The Chinese menu part is near the top, where it explains that to qualify as autistic, a person must have "a total of six (or more) items from (1) (2) and (3), with at least two from (1) and one each from (2) and (3)."

It's a hell of a way to diagnose a person.

By my count, Ezra has nearly all of the symptoms listed, and certainly meets the basic criteria. Yet nowhere does the *DSM* mention sudden, irrational fears. At three years old, that is what Ezra keeps experiencing. He seems to exist in a constant state of heightened anxiety, wary that around every corner could lurk the next Alf doll, another drinking fountain. We never know what will set him off.

He's in the playroom with Ami watching the video of *Toy Story* when suddenly Ezra leaps up from the couch and runs out of the room.

"Turn it off! Turn it *off!*" he's yelling from the hallway, where he has planted his hands firmly on his ears. Ami won't turn the set off, won't even pause the video. Ezra keeps pleading, but won't explain what's wrong. They have not been watching a particularly frightening part of the movie, but Ezra won't go back into the room.

Later, he finds the video's carton and tucks it in the back of a cabinet. Whenever the other boys are contemplating a movie, he won't go near it.

"No *Toy Story*! No *Toy Story*!" he pleads.

Random things incite panic. He receives a birthday gift, a silly children's game called Fishin' Around, featuring magnets players suspend from miniature fishing poles to nab plastic fish from a colorful, rotating disk. It seems an innocuous pastime, but Ezra somehow finds it haunting. He shrieks and moans when he catches sight of it, then shoves it back in its box, safely out of sight. He seems unable to function in its presence.

The irony is that while Ezra is afraid of the fish game and *Toy Story*, he lacks many of the fears he *should* have: He balances precariously on high playground structures; he wanders off to explore the outer limits of the supermarket on his own, not noting or caring that he has lost contact with his mother or father; left unattended for even a second, he wanders into crowds and onto busy streets.

Of all of Ezra's early quirks and idiosyncrasies—the disconnection, the endless repetition, the odd gestures—I find this the most puzzling: his topsy-turvy relationship with fear. Perhaps it's because his fears are so difficult to predict; maybe it's because I feel so powerless to do anything to prevent them or react to them. Like any father, I want to protect my child, but it's difficult to know what I'm protecting him from.

It happens again when he starts at a new preschool. We decide to move him to another local early childhood program, where we have learned that the student-to-teacher ratio is lower and the program seeks out children who have had difficulty fitting in elsewhere.

A few weeks before the new school year is to begin, we get a call from a woman named Dawn who will be working as an aide specifically assigned to Ezra. She wants to visit our home to get acquainted with Ezra a bit and help to ease his entry to the new preschool.

"Tell me about what kinds of things he likes," she asks Shawn over the phone.

"Anything that has to do with Winnie the Pooh," Shawn tells her.

Two days later, on a hot and sunny August afternoon, the doorbell rings and Ami runs to the door. Shawn follows close behind, calling for Ezra to join her.

Dawn walks in. She's in her thirties. She's full of energy, immediately plunking herself down on the hardwood floor in the entryway. Ezra is lingering behind Shawn's leg.

"Are you *Ezra*?" she says with great enthusiasm and flashing a big smile. "I have something really *special* for you!" She holds up a white plastic shopping bag she's brought.

That gets his attention. Walking on his tiptoes, he tilts his head, carefully examining the bag from a few feet away.

"Guess what I *have*?" Dawn says.

The boys all crowd around, trying to guess.

"Can you *guess*?"

Right away, I see that this woman knows how to connect with children. They begin guessing.

"Cookies?" Ami asks.

"Close," she says.

"Ice cream?"

"Even closer!" she says. "What do you think, Ezra?"

Ezra won't guess; he's not playing her game. He just wants her to open the bag.

"Okay," she finally says. "We don't want them to melt." She opens the bag and pulls out a box of popsicles—orange and black in wrappers bearing the likeness of Ezra's favorite character.

"Tigger!" Ezra shouts. He grabs one of the popsicles and launches into the Tigger dance from the movie; then the other boys take theirs, and we move to the back porch, where we sit and Dawn tries to talk to Ezra about the new school, never dropping her energy level even for a second. But he's not listening; instead, he starts sifting through his box of plastic animals.

"Ezra," she says, "your mom and dad and I are talking about you. I'm going to be your teacher when you come to your new school!"

He doesn't respond.

"All the kids are so excited to meet you!"

Shawn and I share a look. It's become rare for us to see adults talking to Ezra. Most give up quickly when they realize he's not looking at them and seems lost in his head.

"I'm not sure he can hear you," Shawn says softly.

"Oh, I know he can," says Dawn.

"I'm not sure he even understands he's going to a new school."

Dawn continues undeterred. "Well, I'll tell you how I look at it," she says. "Some teachers figure, Well, you speak Japanese, and I speak English, so there's no way we can ever communicate. But I want to learn Japanese. I want to learn to speak Ezra's language and communicate with Ezra, so he'll let me into his world. That's what this is all about."

That sounds good to me.

Dawn suggests that we bring Ezra to the preschool a few days before school begins. She wants to give him a chance to explore his new classroom and the playground without any children—to acclimate to the new surroundings without being overwhelmed by the chaos and crowds of the first day. I think of how little fuss he made about entering Karen's classroom a year earlier, but since then he has become increasingly anxious about changes, wary of new situations. He thrives on routine, clings to the known.

On a sunny late August morning, we drive to the low-slung brick preschool complex and meet Dawn at her office. It's decorated with children's art—finger painting and crayon sketches with canary yellow suns and stick-figure children. Her shelves are full of picture books and Slinkys, Crayolas, and modeling clay.

"Hi, Ezra, remember me?" she says with the same warm ebullience she showed at our house. Dawn knows the keys to winning the affection of toddlers: high energy, exaggerated facial expressions, and popsicles. She's full of looks of surprise, over-the-top smiles, and pouty frowns. Ezra is a tough audience, mostly scanning her shelves for toys and occasionally echoing a question.

"I want to show you around your new school, so that when you come next week, you'll know where everything is," she says. "So let's go."

The three of us follow her out the office door and into the courtyard. Ezra spots a large sandbox and immediately collapses, planting himself in the sand and running his fingers through the gray granules.

"Ezra, come on," I say. "That's not what we're—"

"No, it's okay," Dawn says, interrupting. "I want him to make himself at home." She hands him a bucket and shovel. "Let's sit here for a little while, Ezra, and when you're ready, we'll go into the Hungry Caterpillar classroom." She sits down in the sand with him, handing him plastic rakes and scooping at the sand with another trowel. After a few minutes, she asks, "Ready to go visit?" Without hesitation, he tags along behind her.

Good news. He's willing to follow Dawn. She leads us across the small courtyard to a doorway.

"This is going to be your classroom," she says, as the three of us step inside the spacious room, taking in the colorful posters and the toddler-size tables and chairs in a variety of primary colors.

"Look," Dawn says. "Here are the names of all of the kids who are going to be in your class!" She points out a long picture of a friendly-looking green dragon that somebody has painted on butcher paper and hung with masking tape just inside the door. "Can you find your name?"

Shawn and I are just starting to kneel down to help him search when suddenly, without warning, Ezra turns away and sprints out the door, back into the courtyard. It's as if a phantom is chasing after him. It happens so quickly that I'm not sure what startled him. We follow him into the courtyard, where he plants himself behind a wall and around a corner from the classroom.

"What's wrong, sweetie?" Shawn says.

"I don't like that dinosaur!" Ezra says firmly.

"You saw a dinosaur?" I ask.

"I don't like the green dinosaur," he says again. I peek back toward the classroom.

"That's not a dinosaur. It's a friendly dragon, Ezzy," I say. "Let's go back in." But now Ezra is running the other way.

"I'm not going."

Dawn catches up with Ezra. "Sweetheart, that's just a picture with everybody's name. See? Let's go find your name!"

He's not going. Suddenly he's got a look, the same terrified expression that flashed across his face in Dr. Miller's office. And he won't budge. He won't listen to Dawn or Shawn or me. Ezra is not moving.

"That's okay," Dawn says calmly, with the same cheerful voice. "'Cause you know *what*? You're going to come back next week and all the kids are going to be here and they're all going be so excited to meet you!"

Ezra is either not listening or doing a great job of pretending not to listen. He's not looking at Dawn. He's walking in little circles while Dawn keeps talking to him as if he's responding. I would have stopped talking a while ago, figuring that he can't hear, or can't grasp what I am saying. Dawn, though, seems to assume that he can.

Maybe that's what she meant about the Japanese.

The next Tuesday morning, we drive Ezra to the preschool. He's in the car seat in back, wearing maroon sweatpants and a royal blue T-shirt with a picture of Tigger on the chest. Shawn is telling him how exciting it is that he's going to be in a new school. He pulls his hands over his eyes.

"I don't want to see the dinosaur," he says. "No dinosaur!"

"Don't worry about the dinosaur," I say. "It's just a picture."

We walk into the building, but when we get close to the Hungry Caterpillar classroom, he stops. All around us moms and dads are shepherding their sons and daughters inside—little girls in pink tops and pigtails, little boys wearing surfer shorts and colorful T-shirts. Some of the dads are holding camcorders to capture these fleeting moments between summer and fall, between babyhood and the school years. Children are finding their name tags and photos and cubbies and exploring the toys and puzzles and books.

I look down and see Ezra, with fear in his eyes.

"No dinosaur!" he says, turning from the room, just as Dawn is arriving.

"Hi, Ezra! Ready to go in?" she says with a big grin.

He's not. He stands with his lunch box in his hand and walks to the sandbox.

"Come on," I say. "Time to go in."

He won't budge.

I wonder what's truly bothering Ezra. Is this really about the green dinosaur—or dragon, or whatever it is? Or is Ezra terrified by the entire experience: the new school, the unfamiliar teachers, the fresh crop of children? I wonder what he is not telling us—or cannot tell us. Is he experiencing separation anxiety? Is it a fear of losing control? Any of those would be in the realm of normal concerns. My worry is that Ezra's fear is really just about a picture. He's scared of the poster the way he was scared of Alf and the drinking fountain. It's not more complex than that.

In a sense, that's even scarier than any of those more rational explanations. My son isn't anxious about school or making new friends. He's afraid of a crudely drawn dragon painted on a swath of butcher paper.

Dawn follows Ezra to the sandbox.

"You know what?" she says. "I know you're feeling a little bit scared of that dinosaur and maybe you're feeling kind of scared because you're in a new school. So I'm going to sit out here with you for a little while, and then you tell me when you're ready to go in and meet the kids."

Ezra doesn't answer. He's pushing a truck through the sand. I peek through the doorway of the Hungry Caterpillar classroom, where the teachers are trying to hush the children, who sit down in a circle in their parents' laps. One of the teachers begins talking to the group. She's teaching a song, and the kids repeat the verses after her. The sounds waft out the door and window and into the quiet courtyard where Shawn and I are standing, looking over at Ezra sitting in the sandbox with Dawn. I feel torn. Should we go into the classroom with the other kids and parents? Should we stay with Ezra? Dawn can see me looking back and forth.

"We'll be okay, Mom and Dad," Dawn says. "We're going to go in pretty soon."

I shrug and offer a half grin. We both lean over and give Ezra kisses.

"Be good, Ez," I tell him. "It looks really fun in there."

On our way to the parking lot, I see a mom I don't know emerging from a classroom, eyes red from the type of bittersweet tears mothers cry on the first day of school, at the end of a long summer of togetherness.

In the early afternoon, my office phone rings. It's Shawn.

"He never went in," she says.

"What?"

"He wouldn't even go into the classroom. He stayed in the sandbox, and then Dawn took him to her office to play."

"Why didn't she tell him he *had* to go in?" I ask.

"She wants to honor him."

"Honor him?"

"I think she wants it to be his decision."

"Did you tell her that could take forever?"

I learn later what happened: Ezra mostly spent his first day at the new school lingering in the sandbox. When the children in his class spilled out into the yard for recess, he stayed put. The boys and girls climbed on the colorful plastic play structures and grabbed for sand toys and chased one another, squealing, in circles around the handful of trees. Amid it all, Ezra barely took notice, walking his compact circles and talking to himself. When the teachers lined up the children to return to the Hungry Caterpillar room, Dawn tried leading Ezra inside, but he planted his feet firmly: Not going; staying here.

The pattern continues the next day. And the next. I drop off Ezra on my way to work. Dawn meets him at the entrance, with her big smile and booming voice. I wonder all morning what's happening. Shawn phones in the afternoon.

"Oh, my God," she says. "He still won't go in."

I am starting to wonder about the wisdom of this plan.

"If we want a babysitter to watch him play in the sand," I say, only half joking, "we can do that at home and save the commute."

Dawn, for her part, shows no hint of impatience.

"We're going to have a great day, Dad," she says each morning, when I drop him off.

She reports progress, albeit incremental. Ezra is beginning to show more interest in the other children—or at least to acknowledge that there *are* other children. When they go inside after playground time, he lingers near the door and peeks in the windows. The children are curious about him too. One morning, a little blond, blue-eyed girl named Hillary approaches and joins Ezra and Dawn, who draws her into conversation. She sits in the sand with Ezra. They don't talk. When the children line up to go inside, Hillary hesitates and looks at Ezra.

"Come on, Ezra," Dawn says. "Let's follow our friend Hillary!"

He won't. He lets her go, barely looking up as Hillary crosses the yard, glancing back occasionally at the solitary boy in the sand.

"Wanna go?" Dawn urges.

"Dinosaur," Ezra responds.

The next day, a breakthrough. When it's time to return to the classroom, Ezra follows Hillary, at first warily, stepping from the courtyard into the Hungry Caterpillar room like an astronaut stepping cautiously from the lunar capsule onto the surface of the moon. Eyes wide with awe and trepidation, he paces through the room, weaving among the children and scanning the shelves, examining the books, the bins of blocks and stuffed animals, and surveying the floor, with its cushions and beanbag chairs. With hands planted on his ears, he makes his way to a place on the rug, where the children are gathering in a circle and he sits down, with Dawn just behind him.

"Let's all welcome Ezra," says one of the teachers.

Ezra doesn't look up, except occasionally, to check on the green dinosaur and make sure it's not going to attack.

CHAPTER FOUR

The Boy Who Shouted

We learn to live with a child who rarely chooses to converse. Then we begin to encounter a new challenge: Ezra starts communicating.

Shawn and I have grown accustomed to the spacey stares, the questions ignored or mindlessly repeated, and the way Ezra flees any attempt to engage him. We hope and dream for the day our son will begin to open up, to show an interest in reaching out to the world. What we haven't anticipated is what that will mean.

One Saturday morning, I get the answer.

It happens when Ezra is seven, in our neighborhood, which is heavily populated by observant Jews who walk to synagogue on the Sabbath. On any given Saturday morning, a steady stream of pedestrians—nicely dressed, men in yarmulkes, women in long skirts—passes by on the sidewalk in front of our home. We're not Orthodox, but we do observe the Sabbath, and most Saturday mornings, we walk to our synagogue, a little more than a mile away. One Shabbat, I am leaving the house with our three sons at the very moment a neighbor is walking by. Ezra has never met Charlie—I don't know him well myself—but my son immediately notices something about him.

"Why are you so *fat*?" he asks.

Embarrassed, I pretend I didn't hear, and then begin trying to manufacture some small talk about something—*anything*—when Ezra interrupts me, undeterred.

"How did you get so *fat*?" he asks.

Eight thirty on a Saturday morning, and I already have a mess to clean up.

Charlie, a gentle, pleasant man who is indeed on the rotund side, pauses, flummoxed, to contemplate an answer. "I dunno," he says, forcing a smile and patting his belly like a department store Santa. "I . . . I guess I just always liked eating when I was a kid."

Despite my eagerness to flee—preferably to another continent or planet—Charlie is walking the same direction we are. As we stroll past the first few houses, I make every effort to wedge my body between Charlie and Ezra, trying to distract Charlie and head off disaster with idle conversation about the weather, the news headlines, Charlie's children—anything. When it appears that Ezra is about to open his mouth, I shoot him a stern look. Too subtle a hint, apparently, for Ezra.

"Homer Simpson is fat," Ezra says, keeping up his chatter at a volume loud enough to be heard in neighboring states. "Homer Simpson eats a lot of doughnuts."

"Huh?" asks Charlie.

"Ezra!" I plead. *"Stop!"*

"Elephants are fat. Hippos are fat. Pandas are *a little bit* fat."

I stop, kneel on one knee, firmly grab my son's narrow shoulders, draw my face as close as I can to his, and say two words.

"Just . . . *stop!*"

Ami and Noam are behind us, and I can see Ami rolling his eyes and shaking his head. We keep walking, and I try to converse with Charlie, letting the three boys fall behind by a few feet. I hear Ezra continue his chatter—diligently injecting the word *fat* every few seconds—and I desperately endeavor to keep up a conversation with Charlie so he won't hear. After two blocks of this, Charlie is turning onto a side street. Lying, I tell him we are headed in a different direction, and we say good-bye and continue walking—until Charlie disappears from view and I tell Ezra to sit down on the sidewalk while the other boys wait a few feet away.

"Are you *mad*?" he says, a smile on his face. I recognize his involuntary response to being reprimanded. He always smiles, sometimes giggles. It's how he reacts to this kind of confrontation. It makes it more difficult to confront him—his smile makes me feel like laughing myself—but I have to do it.

"I'm *very* angry," I tell him. "Ezra, you don't talk to people like that. That's *not okay*. You shouldn't talk about people's bodies."

He looks down, still grinning slightly. I'm having difficulty judging whether he is actually amused, or just doesn't know how to react.

"Do you understand why?"

"Why?"

I tell him: it makes people feel uncomfortable. It hurts their feelings. It's not polite. People just don't do it.

He looks at me. Silence.

"Ezra," I say, "listen to me. If we're walking, and you see somebody, you don't tell them they're fat."

"Okay! All right!"

"Do you know what you should say to them?"

"What?"

"Just say, 'Shabbat shalom,'" I say, suggesting the traditional Sabbath greeting—the way Jewish people encountering one another in synagogue or on the streets of our neighborhood greet one another. "That's all. 'Hi, Charlie. Shabbat shalom.' You shake hands, like this"—I grab his limp right hand in mine, offering a firm shake to demonstrate how to do—"and that's it. 'Hi, Charlie, Shabbat shalom!'"

"Okay!"

I seem to be getting through. I have learned that sometimes it requires raising my voice just to get his attention.

"Let's practice."

"No."

"Pretend I'm Charlie and you see me. 'Hi, Ezra!' What do you say?"

He is silent.

I wait. "What do you say to Charlie?"

"Shabbat shalom," he says.

"And what about your hand?"

He takes my hand and shakes, looking downward.

"Will you remember that?"

"Yes, can we go now?"

On our twenty-minute walk to synagogue, I pause every few minutes to repeat that question, each time forcefully making my point: *That's not how we talk to people. It hurts their feelings.* I figure that if I repeat it enough, and forcefully enough, I can jar his brain and maybe help Ezra to interrupt his impulse to say the first thing that comes to mind— particularly when he sees anyone who looks a little bit unusual. I don't know whether I am making myself understood, but soon I have an opportunity to find out.

Late that same afternoon, Shawn and I are strolling in the neighborhood with the boys when we cross paths with some friends who are chatting with another couple we have never met. As it happens, the man—sixty or so, in a white shirt and glasses, hands in his trouser pockets—is a bit on the heavy side.

Without warning, Ezra slips away from us and approaches the husband. I feel rising anxiety as he zeroes in.

"Ezra . . ." I start to say. Too late.

"What's your name?" Ezra asks him.

"My name's Jerry," he says, smiling warily.

"Can you take your hands out of your pockets?" Ezra asks.

Jerry, raising an eyebrow, does. Ezra shakes his hand.

"Shabbat shalom," Ezra says.

"Shabbat shalom," Jerry answers.

I'm flushed with a surge of delight—in my son and in my own ability to get through to him, to teach him. I feel a profound sense that anything can be accomplished. Then Ezra, still inches from Jerry, quickly turns around, grins, and looks directly at me.

"See?" he says excitedly, almost shouting with pride. "I didn't say he was *fat!*"

What happens after that is a blur. I do recall a nauseous feeling, a quiet walk home, and the dismal sense that we might never get this right— that raising a child with no intuitive social instinct will be endlessly treacherous, a minefield with unseen disasters lurking everywhere. I have spent the entire morning trying to teach my son a lesson he has completely missed. How, I wonder, will we ever get through?

That night I call a friend who is the mother of an older boy with autism, and recount how my son has managed to insult not one but two fat guys in a single day. She chuckles—clearly she has endured such encounters herself—and then offers advice.

"Our children are concrete thinkers," she explains. "We need to help them to draw connections between specific experiences and general rules." Use this mishap, she suggests, to teach Ezra a more universal idea: that it's not polite to talk *about* other people's bodies, even if you're not talking directly *to* the people.

It sounds like a good plan, and I can say those words to Ezra, but I don't feel that I have the ability to make him understand. Besides, even with our greatest efforts to impart that wisdom, Ezra seems fascinated and drawn to variations in the human physique. Uncensored, he obsessively points out and comments on not just overweight people, but a laundry list of oddities: men's bald scalps, birthmarks on faces, deformed limbs, people in wheelchairs, tattoos, and facial piercings. Like Superman—or a paparazzo—he has an uncanny ability to spot these things from across crowded rooms, up long airplane aisles, in supermarkets from three cash registers away, and through lanes of traffic on busy urban streets. He seems so incapable of withholding comment that his brother Ami develops a sixth sense, his own detector for spotting such people and then steering Ezra out of the way. Waiting at a crosswalk beside his brother, Ami, eagle-eyed, will notice a homeless man in a wheelchair approaching and block Ezra's view with his own body, smiling as he tries to offer distraction.

In a crowded building lobby, I watch Ezra rush up to an elderly woman with a port-wine stain covering half her face. I cringe as Ezra cranes his neck, finally pressing his own face right up to the woman's to get a gander, and dread what he might say.

"You're *old*," Ezra says.

"You're *young*," the woman quips back.

The first day of a new drama program for children with special needs, Ezra manages to contain himself for most of the session. Before it's time to go, the kids, parents, and staffers hold hands in a circle and sing a song. Ezra is antsy, but complies, and then, on his own, he approaches the program's director, a dynamic, tiny woman. I think of what a breakthrough I am witnessing, that without prompting, Ezra might offer his thanks and greetings. Then he puts his hands on her shoulders.

"You are a *not long* person!" he says.

That makes for another extensive conversation on the car ride home. We have talked about weight, not about height.

Or aging.

"You have wrinkly skin," he'll say to the drugstore clerk. "Does that mean you're going to *die* soon?"

Few things escape his notice. Meeting a woman, he'll seem to stare intently for a moment, lost in thought, then say, "You have makeup all over your face."

Lying on the chair at the dentist's office after the hygienist finishes cleaning his teeth, he excitedly—and abruptly—greets the bearded dentist. "Hi, Dr. Bendik! Do you *ever* shave?"

Though some people are taken aback, others find Ezra's honesty to be refreshing. Lacking the impulse to censor his thoughts, he simply speaks the objective truth. As Shawn likes to say, Ezra is the master of uttering what everyone else is thinking.

He's like the little boy in the Hans Christian Andersen tale "The Emperor's New Clothes." In the story, the boy is the hero—the one who articulates what no one else has the nerve to say.

In reality, that kind of honesty is rarely rewarded. I sometimes think about my own difficulty negotiating Shawn's question when she comes home from a shopping excursion with a new outfit, tries it on, and innocently asks, "How does this look on me?" After years of marriage, I still haven't figured out how to finesse that simple query. How will Ezra ever learn to navigate these waters?

As much as I marvel at the honesty of Ezra's compulsive urges to comment on people's appearance, they also make me deeply uncomfortable. In part, that is because his instincts are so jarringly different from my own. If Ezra seems inclined to say whatever comes to mind, unfiltered, I am his opposite. From a young age, I was reserved and shy, particularly with adults.

My instinct is to choose my words carefully—sometimes so carefully that I fail to speak up for fear of misspeaking. I am probably the last person in North America who feels self-conscious about talking on my cell phone in an elevator or any public place. On my morning jogs, I frequently think of the quip I should have made the day before, the comment I wish I had raised in a meeting or in a conversation. That characteristic certainly contributed to my decision to become a writer; my occupation consists largely of pondering the most careful ways to use language.

Though I share his solitary nature, in this sense Ezra is becoming my opposite: Anything that crosses his mind soon crosses his lips.

One afternoon, buckled into his booster seat in the backseat of my Camry, he begins spouting nonsensical words—*fuckus, shick*—and repeating them aloud to himself. From the slight grin on his face—the same expression he had the time I reprimanded him for calling Charlie "fat"—I can tell that he knows there is something vaguely wrong about what he is doing (even though he has deftly found a way to say words that only *resemble* actual cusses), but also that saying those words gives him a certain thrill.

"That's not okay!" I tell him.

"I can't say that?" Ezra asks.

"Nope. You can *think* about that, but don't say it."

"But when *can* I say it?" he asks.

"Never."

"Never? But I *want* to!" He isn't giving up easily. Ezra has already gathered that these words contain a special kind of energy; he wants to use them. "Where *can* I say them?"

Desperate to head off a tantrum, I give him an idea. "Ezra," I say, "you can say those words when you're alone—when nobody else can hear you."

I forget about that conversation until many months later. One July afternoon, we take the kids to a crowded public swimming pool. I lie on a towel beside the large pool, keeping an eye on the boys, who are splashing around among swarms of children enjoying the cool water.

I lose track of Ezra, then spot him, alone in the deeper part of the pool, treading water and occasionally tilting his head forward, submerging his mouth. Panicked that he's having trouble, I dive in and swim quickly to Ezra. I am relieved to find that he is not floundering at all; he is in complete control, and intentionally dipping his mouth just beneath the surface. At first I think he is simply blowing bubbles, but then I get closer and, listening carefully, realize that he is actually speaking. Every few seconds, he dunks his mouth in the water and utters another underwater curse: "Shit!" "Fucker!" "Ass!"

I can't imagine what's going on.

"What are you doing?" I ask.

"You told me," he says, "I could say those words when I'm alone!"

Ezra surely has trouble controlling his impulses, but when he understands the rules, he can learn. What challenge him are the subtleties of what one can and can't say—even if it's true. He tells African-American people their skin is brown. He reminds acquaintances repeatedly that their loved ones have died—and what, exactly, they died from.

"Grandpa Jack, he passed away from cancer—you're very sad," he tells a family friend on a dozen different occasions.

"George died; he was very old," he reminds another friend, months— even years—after her dog was put down.

He has become hyperaware that he is Jewish, and curious who else is. With so much talk in our house about things Jewish—holidays and synagogues and rabbis and schools—he comes to think of this as fair game. It begins with repeated questions he asks Shawn and me: "Is Thanksgiving Jewish or Christian?" he'll ask. He has the same question about the Fourth of July, Halloween, countries, and fictional characters. It's usually focused on borderline concepts; he's trying to figure out the world and it's unsettling to him when things or people don't fit neatly into categories. As with most of his habits and quirks, at first I perceive this new preoccupation as a sign of progress, an indication that Ezra has achieved a new level of awareness. Soon, though, it crosses over into the territory of very annoying behavior. How many times can I answer the same Thanksgiving question?

"Is Thanksgiving a Jewish or Christian holiday?"

"Both. It's American."

"Is it Jewish or Christian?"

"Both."

"It's Jewish *and* Christian."

"That's right, Ezra."

"Thanksgiving is Jewish *and* Christian."

After a while, his chatter is not so much about getting the information as it is about repeating the question, and then the answer, stimulating himself through the act of reiterating.

And then he crosses yet another boundary. We're at Ralphs, the grocery store, and the cashier asks how our day is going.

"Are you Jewish?" Ezra responds. The man shakes his head and smiles.

I'm not sure where the question is coming from. But it becomes one of his standard lines. Ezra asks our gardener, people walking their dogs in the neighborhood, his gym teacher, a waiter at an Italian restaurant. He doesn't seem to have plans for what to do with the answers. He simply likes to ask.

I see the questions as positive developments, for two reasons: He is gaining an awareness of religion and what it means. And at least he's not asking why they're fat.

When he meets people with any signs of gray hair or wrinkles, he gets into the habit of asking them their ages, then issuing one of two responses: "*Oooh*, you're *middle aged!*" or "*Oooh*, you're *old!*"

I suggest that it would be better merely to tell people they're looking well. He tries that, and it's an improvement, though he throws so much enthusiasm into it—"You look *great!*"—that he leaves some people feeling a bit unsettled. Just as reading facial expressions doesn't come naturally, neither does understanding tone of voice or knowing how to moderate the tenor of his delivery. His speech often sounds stiff and unnatural.

Sometimes his reactions reveal how he is puzzling over things he doesn't grasp. After a couple we know splits up, every time we spend time with the woman, Ezra asks where her ex-husband is.

"He doesn't live here anymore," Beth patiently reminds him on each occasion. "We're divorced, remember?"

The next time Ezra sees the ex, it's at his daughter's bat mitzvah, at a dramatic moment when he's carrying the Torah scroll up the synagogue's center aisle. Spotting the familiar face, Ezra dashes to the aisle and plants himself directly in the path, halting the entire procession.

"Ronnie!" he says. "You're divorced now! You live in a *new* house!"

While Ronnie tries to smile and make the best of it, I reach out an arm like a vaudeville hook, quickly extricating my son from the scene, planting him back on his seat next to me. I glare at him, but Ezra merely looks perplexed—then slowly seems to realize what he's done.

"Was that like saying he was *fat*?" he asks.

"Not exactly," I say, smiling. "But close."

When Ezra is about eleven, Shawn has scheduled an appointment at the house for a project she is working on with a woman who happens to be both obese and rather short. That morning the doorbell rings. I listen from upstairs as Ezra dashes to the front door to see who is there. I run to intervene, but not quickly enough. From the hallway, I watch him swing open the door, catch sight of Cathy, suddenly gasp, and then cover his mouth with his right hand. I greet Cathy and point her toward

Shawn. As she walks past me and inside, Ezra, still standing near the door, speaks to me in a stage whisper.

"I didn't say *anything*."

I tell him I am proud of him.

I can sense it was difficult for him, but slowly Ezra is learning.

Not long after that he is telling me about playing a board game at school with a teacher and another student. The boy's name sounds familiar, but I'm not certain which kid he is.

"Matthew," I say. "That's the really tall kid, right?"

Ezra stares at me, bug-eyed, a surprised grin flashing across his face.

"What?" I ask, not understanding what he's thinking.

He is silent.

"What is it?"

Finally he erupts. "You talked about his *body*!"

I ponder that for a moment, and realize something about my son: Every deficit comes with a gift. In this case, his challenge is coming to understand the subtle nuances of talking to—and about—other people. The gift, however, is an honesty and openness that other people will always envy. After all, is there a rational explanation for why we favor tall people over short people, the slender over the obese? Shawn and I have the task of helping our son to navigate the arbitrary, sometimes counter-intuitive rules of social engagement. In the meantime, like the boy in "The Emperor's New Clothes," Ezra is teaching us a thing or two about telling the truth.

CHAPTER FIVE

Finding My Son at the Zoo

With his difficulty mastering the complexities of what one should and shouldn't say to people about their bodies, it's no wonder that Ezra is drawn to animals. You can call a giraffe tall with impunity. You can say all you want about how fat the hippo is without hurting anyone's feelings.

In fact, Ezra has been attracted to the idea of animals from early on, becoming so enamored with a friend's plastic jungle animals as a toddler that we gave him some of his own—zebras, a lion, and a tiger—for his second birthday. Another child might have employed the figures in imaginary play—say, acting out dramatic, violent interactions between the lion and his prey. Not Ezra. As a toddler—before we truly grasped his differences—he would haul around his growing collection of animals and dinosaur figures to the brick back patio of our Los Angeles home, spending long hours lining up the creatures in precise, symmetrical patterns as Shawn and I watched, feeling a combination of amazement and bewilderment.

Occasionally Noam or Ami would knock a rhino or stegosaurus out of place—or grab one for their own play—and elicit a fit of uncontrollable screaming from Ezra, who was tortured at his precise formation being broken.

"It's all right, Ezzy," Shawn would say, crouching down and trying to put the creatures back in place, but it was impossible to placate him. He seemed to be following a rigid system in his own mind, and only he could fix the problems.

At age three, he singles out a three-inch-long wooden alligator from a jigsaw puzzle as his special companion, then designates a similarly sized plastic toy alligator as another. For months, he goes everywhere—the playground, the bathtub—clutching one alligator in each hand. Soon after, he adds a foot-long plastic crocodile he keeps nearby at all times. Other children have security blankets. He has security reptiles.

That causes its own set of problems. Our family is setting out to visit my parents in Portland when an airport security screener peeks into Ezra's Elmo backpack and begins shaking her head sternly. I can't imagine what the problem is, until she points at the larger plastic crocodile inside.

"He can't carry that on," she says sternly.

"He *has* to," Shawn replies, smiling. "We don't have a choice."

The woman shakes her head again. She explains that it is forbidden to carry a replica of anything that would be illegal on a plane—guns, bombs, crocodiles.

"Come *on*," I plead. "It's a toy."

Never have parents begged with such persistence for a green hunk of plastic to be allowed onto an airplane, but the woman won't relent.

"Crocodile!" Ezra screams, reaching for the toy. Shawn tries to comfort him while I rush back to the airline counter, trying to skip the lengthy line of stone-faced business commuters and explain to a clerk why I am in such a hurry to check a pint-size *Sesame Street* backpack and return to my family.

Ezra's strong attraction to animals becomes something deeper when the wildlife is real. One autumn Sunday, when he is still three, Shawn and I pile the boys into the Toyota minivan and drive to Griffith Park, where the Los Angeles Zoo stretches over eighty acres of gently sloping hills. Our afternoon with our three young children among the flamingos and meerkats feels to me like a lovely but ordinary family outing, but it is igniting something new within Ezra.

This shows up soon after, when he is taking his evening bath and I notice him reciting a long list of animals to himself: "Tiger . . . bear . . . rhinoceros . . . hippo. . . ." Following along, I suddenly realize what he is doing: ticking off the names of the animals in the exact order we saw them at the zoo.

The next time we return to Griffith Park, he announces most of the animals even before we have arrived at an exhibit. At the seals: "*Now* let's go see the polar bears." At the polar bears: "*Now* it's time for the otters." Just as with his animal patterns in the backyard, the combination of rigid order and wild animals stimulates him.

So we keep going back.

At times, I wonder if it is the animals he is attracted to, or just the order. After school one afternoon, I visit the zoo with Ezra, who is so eager that he pulls my arm to get as quickly as possible from the car to the gate. Then he dashes on his regular circuit through the zoo, barely pausing. I feel baffled by the behavior and upset at how disconnected he seems. On the drive home, I ask Ezra why he didn't stop to look at the animals.

Silence.

"I thought we came here to look at the giraffes and the lions and gorillas," I say. "What were you doing?"

As we make our way through downtown traffic, he is silent again for a few moments and then says something just audible: "I saw them."

Yes. But I can't fathom what could explain his rush.

Not long after that we are at a local children's museum that has an interactive Noah's Ark exhibit, including large buckets of the plastic animals Ezra so enjoys. While the other boys circulate through the various displays and activities, Ezra spends the entire hour picking through the animals, dividing them by species and size in the toy ark's small compartments. It strikes me that this is exactly what has been drawing Ezra to the zoo. He has cataloged all the species in his mind. He draws comfort from finding them where they are supposed to be: the koalas in their tree, the lemurs in their cage, the elephants wandering their grounds. Nearly everywhere else he goes, my son is filled with anxiety. Human beings can be unpredictable and scary, with their social rules and their subtle facial expressions. But the giraffes don't ask questions, and the chimps don't care what you say about them. Ezra doesn't merely want to see animals; he wants to live in this mannered world, with its patterns and structures and where there are no surprises.

On another afternoon I encourage him to walk slowly, and I hang back to see what he will do. We arrive at the sea lions just as a zookeeper brings a pail of fish for lunch. Ezra leans on the metal rail and gazes for half an hour, entranced, watching the keeper toss fish. He's fascinated with how the creatures swim for their food, crawling in and out of the pool. I think of how Ezra can barely sit at the cafeteria table, how he endures karate lessons only while asking his instructor every two minutes when the hour will be up. As I watch him smile with delight, I feel a profound sense of hope mixed with sadness—hope that he has found something that brings him such pleasure, sadness that he hasn't shown that kind of focused engagement with other people.

Instead of letting his passion for animals become yet another lonely avenue, I decide to make it the foundation of a connection between the two of us. I find myself making the trek to Griffith Park as frequently as I can. Elsewhere, Ezra can be a tangle of tics and repetitive motions, uttering snippets of video dialogue, and hiding out under blankets or mattresses. At the zoo, all of that melts away. I let him flash our membership card, we pass through the familiar gates, and I watch him sprint to the sea lions, morphing within minutes into a different boy: calm, open, and happy.

"Oh, *there's* the little ocelot. You see it?" he says, a lilt in his voice, eyes wide with innocent delight.

Friends tease me, curious about how a grown man could spend so much time watching koalas chew on leaves. But I never tire of watching my son, never get bored with the way the zoo transforms him. I cherish those sixty or ninety minutes in which I can connect with Ezra and we can fit in with the crowds, just like any other father and son.

And I feel continually surprised by the revelations that come from Ezra's fascination with animals. Long after Ami and even Noam have out-grown their interest in zoo visits—as most children do—Ezra's attraction just soars.

For Ezra's tenth birthday, Shawn's brother and his wife send him a book that might have come straight out of Ezra's dreams. *Animal: The Definitive Visual Guide to the World's Wildlife* is a seven-and-a-half-pound, 624-page visual encyclopedia of nearly every animal on the planet. Ezra adopts the hefty volume, with its cover close-up of a mandrill's colorful face, as his constant companion. On Saturday mornings, he silently pores over it in synagogue as if it were the Torah itself. On the school bus, while other kids chat or stare off, Ezra inhales data about habitats and extinction rates. I come to think of it as my son's way of bringing the zoo along with him.

Not long after that, during another visit to Portland, my father takes a morning off from work to bring Ezra and me to the Oregon Zoo. As the three of us make our way, Dad grows amused and enchanted by his grandson's enthusiasm and knowledge. We are in a complex of squat buildings housing the primates when Dad looks into one cage.

"What kind of monkey is that?" he asks.

"That's not a monkey; it's a siamang, the largest gibbon—lower risk of extinction," Ezra tells him, moving on quickly to the next exhibit.

Dad surreptitiously pulls out his cell phone and accesses the Internet. "He's right!" he says with a delighted grin. I feel gratified that my father has shared the kind of moment I have experienced so often with Ezra, an instant of grasping and celebrating what makes his grandson unique.

Ezra doesn't simply remember the animals. He has a remarkable recall of his interactions with them.

At nine years old, he is reading aloud to me from a book that mentions a character's favorite bird. I take the opportunity to ask him his.

"A woodpecker," he says.

I ask him if he has ever seen a woodpecker.

"No," he says. "But I've heard one, when we were on a hike on November twenty-eighth, 2003. It was a Friday."

He is, of course, correct. A year and a half earlier, friends joined us for an outing in Malibu the day after Thanksgiving. Ezra asked that morning about the ticking sound he kept hearing echoing through the woods. I wasn't aware that he had tucked away the memory.

In fact, he has accumulated an extensive mental diary of such moments, whose entries he shares spontaneously at random moments, over pizza or in the car. His are not mere fleeting memories. They seem to transport him back to the place and time, as if Ezra is reliving the sights and sounds and even the feelings he had inside. "Remember at the Santa Barbara Zoo in November of 2005," he says over his oatmeal, breaking into laughter, "when that baby threw her daddy's hat in to the otters?"

He giggles loudly and recounts again and again the time at a zoo when he happened upon the sun bear exhibit just in time to spot one of the bears urinating. Like any preadolescent, he finds the thought of a peeing animal endlessly funny. He smiles when he remembers the time Shawn's parents, then living in Ohio, brought him and his brothers to visit a farm, where an unruly goose made its presence known with loud and persistent honking.

But the memories aren't all good. Once, on a visit to a small zoo in rural Big Bear, California, we arrive at an enclosure of owls just after they have been offered a luncheon of dead white mice. For months and years after, I can see him struggle on occasion to block the memory from his brain. Even hearing mention of the name of the zoo makes him physically agitated—so much so that he covers his ears, closes his eyes, and says, "Stop-stop-stop-stop-*stop!*"

Possessing a superhuman memory has its drawbacks; when he wants to shake an unpleasant recollection, it can prove difficult.

Yet, with the exception of those rare, painful images, I can sense that Ezra is accumulating a storehouse full of joyous memories that he carries with him, just as he lugs the hefty animal book around. The familiar paths of the Los Angeles Zoo (and the other zoos he visits) provide a happy place—not school, where he struggles to focus and make sense of the rules; not home, where he can work himself into a frenzy with his repetitious habits. At the zoo, his soul seems serene.

I am building my own memories as well, forging a deep connection with my son through the simple sharing of experiences. The more we visit the zoo, the closer I feel to him, and the more I marvel at his struggles, his worries, his quirks, and his wondrous mind. Without setting out to do so, I have discovered a place and a way to connect with Ezra.

Not everyone shares my delight. In his excitement to see the black-necked swans one day when he is ten, Ezra jostles his way past an older man and inadvertently plants himself directly in front of the man's son, blocking the child's view.

"*Excuse* me!" the man says.

Ezra, oblivious to such social nuance, just keeps gazing.

"Do you *mind*?" the man continues.

He doesn't. "Abba, you see the swan?" Ezra says—still not noticing the man, and now outing me as his escort. The man glares at me.

"He could say, 'Excuse me'!" the man says.

I have an answer prepared for such situations, but I never actually trot it out. I imagine myself stepping over, putting my face right in his, narrowing my eyes, and unloading. "Mister," I say, "it's a miracle that kid can speak at all." That would be followed by a lecture on the neurological underpinnings of autism and a sob story about my son's journey through special education and a series of doctors and therapists, and conclude with a final admonition: "I think *you're* the one who should say, 'Excuse me'!"

That's what I dream of saying. Instead, I follow Ezra's lead: I ignore the man and watch the animal. (Occasionally, I wonder whether it might be better in such situations to educate strangers by patiently explaining what makes my son different. But I usually err on the side of letting people experience a different type of person, unfiltered.)

"Yes, I see it!" I say, looking at the swan. "It's *beautiful*, isn't it?"

By then, Ezra has slipped through the crowd and I trail him as he scurries off toward the Chinese alligator, blissfully unaware of the disgruntled gentleman he is leaving behind.

Even when he isn't bumping into people, Ezra can stand out. There simply aren't many children his size at the zoo cooing so excitedly and loudly over the animals. He has never really learned sensitivity about controlling the volume of his voice, even in places like movie theaters and restaurants, so he certainly isn't going to learn that among the Sunday throngs crowding the paved paths of the L.A. Zoo. Ezra has developed a particular affection for otters and lemurs, both species that seem to share his playful and gentle nature. Seeing the otters so excites him that on some visits he stands at their enclosure literally bouncing on his toes with glee and excitedly reciting one factoid after another for every passerby to hear: "Those are otters! Otters are mammals! They're in the same family as weasels, badgers, and skunks! My favorite kind is the North American river otter and also the sea otter!" He seems more delighted with each new detail, and other visitors must wonder whether perhaps this little boy works here in some capacity. "They're carnivores! They like to eat fish! They're very playful!" I have heard this litany over and over, though sometimes he surprises me by adding a new piece of information: "Otters live on every continent except Australia and Antarctica!"

One afternoon when he is eleven he's watching the sifaka lemurs, pacing and hopping in his orange fleece jacket as he mimics the movements of the animals bouncing inside the cage. "I love these guys!" he squeals. "They're *soooooo cuuuute*." Other visitors come and go: moms pushing strollers, a den of Cub Scouts. Occasionally I catch a couple of them exchanging looks, as if to say, "What's *wrong* with that kid?"

Once self-conscious and worried, I have learned from Ezra to ignore those glances. Like Ezra, I leave my troubles and concerns at the zoo gate, letting go of worries about money or work and losing myself in the animals and our shared moments.

As much as I cherish that link, I do sometimes wonder whether Ezra might ever find another child with whom to share the experience, a friend to make his existence that much less solitary. One Sunday when Ezra is ten, Shawn has joined us at the zoo when a woman about my age approaches us.

"I think my son knows your son from school," she says.

Ezra does recognize the boy, an awkward ten-year-old who, it turns out, shares his passion for animals and the zoo. The boy is carrying a digital camera, and shows us how he likes to catalog the animals, stopping at each exhibit to photograph the informational sign, then the animals inside. His mother explains to us how he prints the photos and assembles them into albums he likes to flip through at home.

Shawn suggests we walk together, and I feel excited at the idea that Ezra can reach out to a schoolmate and bond over their mutual enthusiasm for wildlife. I imagine playdates at the zoo, hours to be spent musing over the boy's photo albums and Ezra's big book. But the two boys just trudge on, taking note of the dromedaries and gray wolves, but oblivious to each other. I am disappointed, but then I look at Ezra, who is unfazed, eager to get to the zebras.

Occasionally the zoo affords us sublime moments I couldn't have experienced anywhere else or with anyone else. One chilly, misty afternoon when Ezra is eight, he notices that a new exhibit that has been under construction has finally opened. As we get close, Ezra leads me to a side of the enclosure where the floor of the cage is at about his eye level. We are the only visitors nearby, and Ezra quickly spots the animal inside: a young snow leopard—gorgeous, white with black spots—pacing back and forth inside the cage. Ezra squeezes his cheek up to the metal enclosure, tracing the leopard's steps with his eyes.

"Listen," I tell him.

We are so close, and the place is so quiet, that I can hear the leopard rhythmically inhaling and exhaling.

"He's breathing!" Ezra says.

As the leopard paces, Ezra lines up his body with the animal's, mimicking its steps, pacing back and forth, again and again. The air is cool and I see the vapor from the leopard's breath.

"What's that?" Ezra asks. "What's coming out of him?"

"You can see his breath," I tell him.

Ezra stops pacing and places his hands on the fence between himself and the creature. He takes a few deep breaths, and then I realize what he is doing: Watching the vapor emerging from the leopard, he is adjusting his own breath to be in sync with the cat's. I take a few steps back and watch my son—who has gone through life seemingly so alone, who would never think of pacing the playground with another child— breathing in near silence with a leopard. I savor the moment, satisfied that I have brought Ezra to a place where he can be, at least for two minutes, content and calm, at peace.

And then he darts away, on to the next animal and the next and the next, until it is time to head to the parking lot. He senses the change, and even before we exit the gate, he starts in again on the usual chatter about Disney movies and junk food. As we walk hand in hand out toward the car, I wonder if the joy Ezra feels among his animals will ever permeate the rest of his life—and hope my little boy might someday feel as content and comfortable among his own species.

CHAPTER SIX

The Reader

We're at Brad and Elana's house when Ezra is five years old. The four adults are chatting over what's left of lunch. Meanwhile, most of the kids have scattered around the house, occupying themselves with a bucket of Legos and the chocolate-chip ice cream that has appeared on the kitchen counter. Ezra sits on the floor nearby doing what he spends much of his time lately doing: obsessively paging through a picture book, front to back, then back to front. It's not idle page turning. He holds the book close to his face, examining the letters and images the way some kids stare at their Game Boys. This afternoon it's his current book of choice: a simple, colorful storybook about Thomas the Tank Engine.

Elana glances toward him.

"Is he reading yet?" she asks.

I am not sure I've heard correctly.

"Reading?" I ask. She might as well have asked if he's composing symphonies. But she's serious. Ezra, thanks to *Sesame Street*, can recognize the letters, but he shows no sign of stringing them together into words. In school he is so challenged by the simple act of paying attention that it's hard to imagine him achieving much more. Brad and Elana have an older son with a diagnosis similar to Ezra's. Often, Elana has valuable advice and insights. But this time I can't fathom what she's thinking.

"Yeah," she says. "I'll bet he's reading."

Elana is smiling cryptically as she says it, and I wonder if she's speaking in some sort of coded, ironic language, as if she's putting quotation marks around the word *reading*. Is this her way of saying that maybe Ezra thinks he's reading, but of course we all know better than that? Surely Elana can't be implying that Ezra could be comprehending the words on the page.

He does spend countless hours—the majority of some days—scrutinizing the pages of books: Dr. Seuss, *The Story of Babar, Madeline.* He seems magnetically attracted to their pages, mesmerized by their images and practically hypnotized by the process of opening, staring, and flipping page after page after page. It may be a form of imitation. He's growing up in a home lined with bookshelves, with a rabbi for a mom and a writer for a dad. The way other kids might put on an apron and pretend to cook or sit behind the wheel and play bus driver, Ezra flips through books, just like his parents. Yet with all of that, it has never occurred to me that at the age of five my son is actually reading those words.

"He does love books," I say. "But I don't think he's . . . *reading.*"

"Here," Elana says. "Let me see." She rises from the table, taking a place next to Ezra on the floor. She sits cross-legged beside him, examining the book he's holding.

"Let's read this," she says, and she squeezes next to him, pointing at one word at a time, pausing to listen to Ezra. I watch, waiting for a miraculous breakthrough, the moment my five-year-old boy suddenly emerges from his two-year-long trance to reveal his hidden ability.

It doesn't happen.

Instead, he merely continues to page through, staring at the book. And as we continue our conversation with Brad, I let the momentary fantasy slip away.

Until a few minutes later, when Elana returns to the table.

"He's reading," she says evenly, still wearing her mysterious smile.

"What do you mean?" I ask. It just doesn't make sense. I feel confused and skeptical—and it must show on my face.

"He's *smart*," she says. "Of *course* he can read."

Later, on the way home, Shawn and I are both quiet for a while, and then I ask my wife: "Do you think he's reading?"

She shakes her head. "Do I think he *will* read—someday? Yes," she says. "Is he now?" She shakes her head again.

I don't know what to think. Have we missed something? Have we been overlooking new developments all along? Has Ezra been reaching fresh milestones, higher levels of comprehension, unprecedented accomplishments that have escaped our notice? Has he been deciphering the words on the pages all this time, while we naively dismissed his page turning as mere habit? I'm perplexed. Did Ezra actually *read* the words on the page to Elana? Or is she just trying to send us a signal—that we ought to have faith in our son, ought to assume that he is a mindful, intelligent person?

That night at bedtime, I sit on the boys' bedroom floor with Ezra, an Eric Carle picture book between the two of us. I point to a word and ask him to read it to me.

Silence.

I read it, then point to the next.

No response.

"*Read* to me!" he demands.

"No," I say. "You read to *me*."

He squirms. "*Read*, Abba!"

"You," I say.

It's silent. In the hush between us I am aware of the tension within myself—the tug-of-war between acceptance and aspiration, between embracing what my son is and pushing him toward what he might become. As much as I aim to appreciate Ezra on his own terms, with all of his eccentricities and limitations, Elana's comment has touched a part of me that dreams for—maybe even expects—my son to do what any other child could do: make friends, sit still, read books.

While I try to rein in those too-grand thoughts, he takes me by surprise. Soon after that evening Ezra magically starts spelling words.

At first it's his own name: E-Z-R-A. And within a few weeks he has added to that the names of his brothers: A-M-I-E-L (Ami's full name) and N-O-A-M. He spells what he calls me: A-B-B-A, and what he calls Shawn: I-M-A.

One night, I'm making dinner in the kitchen and notice Ezra running into the room and grabbing the brightly colored plastic magnetic letters from the refrigerator door. Again and again he appears in the doorway, hurries to the fridge, grabs a letter in each hand, then scampers back out. When he leaves and doesn't return, I peek into the playroom next door to see what's up, and spot Ezra arranging letters in the corner of the small table that holds his wooden trains and tracks. He has placed eight letters into a crooked line to spell a word: D-I-N-O-S-A-U-R.

A big word for a little boy who seems so lost in his own head.

"Did *you* do that?" I ask.

He beams: "I spelled *dinosaur*! That's how you spell *dinosaur*!"

I smile and watch my son fiddle with the letters and the trains and wonder what else is going on behind his deep brown eyes. And for a moment I ponder another question: Was Elana right? Is Ezra teaching himself? And I wonder whether he has been doing that all along—and whether he just might continue.

Soon, spelling becomes yet another obsession. When Ezra is not mimicking phrases from *Winnie the Pooh* or disgorging minutiae about Thomas, he is asking how to spell words: names, characters, objects, animals. This is what he fills the silence with now as we drive around with Ezra strapped in his car seat in the back of my Toyota.

"How do you spell *tiger*? . . . How do you spell *house*? . . . How do you spell *Mickey*?"

Ezra's newfound spelling prowess earns him a modest reputation among our children's friends. Some neighbors install a backyard trampoline, which quickly gains popularity among the younger kids, who line up to bounce together within the circular netted enclosure. Ezra, in particular, finds the repetitive leaping motion so comforting that we begin making routine visits. Jumping within the twelve-foot circle provides exercise that calms Ezra, wears him out, and leaves him feeling more centered.

One afternoon I'm sitting on a patio chair near the trampoline when I notice that a couple of the younger kids have spontaneously developed a game: asking Ezra to spell as he jumps.

"Listen! Listen!" one girl of eight or nine is telling her sister. "Do it again!"

She bounces in sync with Ezra, shouting one word at a time. He repeats the word, then spells it, one letter per bounce. The children crowd around—as much as they can while springing up and down—to listen, fascinated and impressed by the little boy who cannot hold a conversation and won't join in a basketball game but can magically jump and spell *dinosaur*.

He can spell. Does that mean he can read? Learning is such a mysterious process in any child—all the more so in a child who cannot—or will not—communicate about what he is learning. Ezra is building a remarkable mental catalog of spelling words, but can he make sense of words from seeing them? We simply don't know.

That is, until an evening a few months later. It's Yom Kippur, the holiest day on the Jewish calendar—and the longest synagogue day of the year. We're in Redlands, the small city east of Los Angeles where Shawn works as occasional visiting rabbi for a small, tight-knit community. At nightfall, after twenty-four hours of prayer and fasting, I'm eagerly anticipating the day's end. As my wife and the cantor lead the congregation in chanting the climactic final Hebrew prayers, volunteers are busy laying out noodle kugels and fruit salads on tables in the rear of the hall for a potluck meal to break the fast. Finally, a long blast of a ram's horn—the shofar—marks the holiday's end, and the hundred or so famished congregants descend on the buffet tables, eagerly filling paper plates with food. Amid the crowd, I'm trying to assemble plates for the boys and Shawn, when suddenly a piercing sound rings out.

BRRRRRRRIIIIIIINNNNNNNNGGGGGGG!

Looking up, I see a strobe light flashing near a large red cone-shaped speaker mounted on a high wall.

BRRRRRRRIIIIIIINNNNNNNNGGGGGGG!

I look around for smoke or flames, thinking perhaps a careless kitchen volunteer set a burner too high and scorched a blintz casserole. But I see no smoke, no fire.

Moms and dads scurry to find their children and rush toward the doors while balancing plates and cups. Fire or no fire, after going hungry for a day, nobody wants to abandon the potato salad midbite.

Suddenly, a man's booming voice rises above the din: "It was the rabbi's son."

I can tell from the tone which one he means. *That* son.

In the midst of the confusion, I spot Ezra. He's in a corner, clasping his forearms against his ears and leaning forward, head almost to his knees. He uncoils now and then for just long enough to peer at the dessert table, with its trays of brownies and home-baked coffee cakes.

I notice a couple of congregants examining a red alarm box on the wall, its handle protruding at an odd angle. One man props himself up on a folding chair and holds a gray plastic trash bin over the blaring speaker to muffle the sound; he's only partially successful.

"It's all right!" the man shouts over the alarm. "There's no fire."

It's too late. As the confused crowd debates whether to stay or go, I grab Ezra, who is still holding his ears, and nudge him outside, only to encounter *another* siren, this one on the red fire engine that's arriving at the curb. A pair of firefighters in full gear descend and head inside. Ezra, practically shaking from the commotion, is also mesmerized by the red truck, with its pulsating light.

"Let's go, sweetheart," I say, placing an arm around him as we walk down the block, away from the people and the noise and the fading scent of kugel and toasted bagels. Around the corner and finally away from the blaring siren, I tell him he can take his hands off his ears. He still won't. I pull his hands off of them myself, hold them in mine, and try to catch his eye.

"Ez, did you touch something?"

He doesn't respond.

"Ezzy, what did you do?" I ask.

He finally answers: "I touched that box."

"Why did you do that?" I ask.

He says four words: "It said, 'Pull Down.'"

I gaze up the block at the fire engine and its flashing light, the adults and kids lingering around the doorway balancing paper plates loaded with food and clutching cups of orange juice. And I look at Ezra, at once feeling exasperated and tickled, simultaneously experiencing bewilderment and awe. At the end of this long day of fasting and family, of prayer and reflection, I have stumbled upon a revelation: My son can read.

He can, but will he? Just as he did in preschool, Ezra often keeps a book nearby as a sort of talisman. When he begins riding a bus to school, he lugs along books to provide comfort and ease the transition between home and classroom. He insists on carrying a different one each day. Occasionally, he breaks his own rule inadvertently, realizing when he is a stride or two out the door that the book in his hands is a repeat from yesterday or last week, and then quickly turning around to rush back inside.

"I need a book!" he says, slight panic in his voice.

I try handing him whatever I come across near the door—a picture book, a volume of animal photos, a silly pop-up book.

"No, I need a *different* book," he fusses.

"It's all right," I assure him. "Take this one."

"No!" he groans, rushing past me, toward his bedroom. He disappears and I shrug and signal apologies to the bus driver. Ezra emerges with the book he wants—there is a method to all of this, an order that only he understands. From the doorway I watch him run toward the bus with his red backpack over his shoulder and *Dr. Seuss's ABC* under his arm.

Some children need their ragged blankets nearby; some, their favorite Barbies. Ezra—who once favored a plastic crocodile—now requires a book.

Yet as he gets older, the comfort he finds in the physical objects is matched by the discomfort he seems to encounter in his struggles to read. Ezra can readily decipher the combinations of letters, but his understanding of the words and ideas seems to lag.

On a doctor's advice, we enroll him in an expensive remedial program aimed at children who share his difficulty connecting words and meaning. It's an intensive one-on-one approach, with four-hour days, a fresh tutor arriving every sixty minutes to implore Ezra repeatedly to create mental images to match the words in selected passages.

"What are you picturing for *iceberg*?" a tutor asks.

"What are you picturing for *car*?" inquires another.

"Tell me what you're picturing for *baking*," says a third.

Ezra, miserable, begins repeatedly posing a question of his own: "When are they going to stop asking me what I'm picturing?"

To his relief, with little apparent evidence of improvement, we pull him out of the program.

Finally, in the third grade, he gets the teacher he needs. That year, Shawn has arranged for a sabbatical, taking a leave from her duties at the university where she teaches. Her plan is to focus on some research and writing projects she has long hoped to accomplish. That November, she attends an autism conference in Washington, D.C., where she feels overwhelmed and inspired by meeting other parents and by what she learns at session after session about therapies, education, and medical developments. Back home, Ezra has been floundering and unhappy in his

public school special-education class. From her hotel room, she phones to
report an epiphany.

"I looked at my date book, and I have no appointments in the month
of December—nothing," she tells me.

"And?" I ask.

"And I think I should homeschool Ezra."

"For December?"

"For the rest of the school year," she says. "He needs us."

It's a radical idea, but it immediately makes so much sense that I offer
little resistance. Ezra's school situation isn't working, and Shawn is a
natural and gifted educator with time suddenly on her hands.

I watch as she patches together a curriculum and a team, securing a
tutor to help with math and science, and adding sessions with a gym
teacher who already knows Ezra. Shawn focuses on literacy, encouraging
our son to read aloud with her every day. Often this provokes a tantrum,
with Ezra moaning and dramatically sobbing, throwing his body to the
floor in protest when she tries to slide next to him on the couch for him
to read.

Part of the challenge is choosing the appropriate material. She has
some luck with a series about a brother and sister whose tree house
becomes a time machine, mysteriously transporting them to the Civil
War era or ancient Egypt. They take turns reading. The simple prose and
illustrations hold his attention, at least momentarily, and Shawn writes
questions for Ezra to answer after each short chapter to demonstrate his
comprehension.

After some initial promise, though, her reception isn't much better
than what the tutors were getting.

"No more tree house!" he protests.

"Well, what do you want to read?" she asks.

He doesn't answer, but later that day, he is flipping through a children's book called *Whiteblack the Penguin Sees the World*, a posthumously published storybook by the authors of the Curious George series. Seizing on his interest, Shawn makes that the next day's reading material. Somehow—maybe because the illustrations are so plentiful and most of the characters are animals—Ezra is willing to read the book without hesitation or protest. Snuggling on the sofa next to his mother, he reads about Whiteblack, a penguin who has run out of stories to tell and who embarks on a series of adventures aimed at finding new material. Of course, everything goes wrong: His canoe hits an iceberg; he falls asleep in a cannon and gets shot into the sea; he gets tangled in a fishing net.

Ezra is enthralled by the misadventures.

"What do you notice about Whiteblack?" Shawn asks.

"He makes a lot of mistakes," Ezra says.

"That's right!" says Shawn. "Why does he do that?"

"Why does he do that?" Ezra repeats.

"Why do you think he does that?"

"He's different from everybody."

"Yes," she says. "Do you know anybody who's a little bit different like that?"

"I'm different," he says.

"How are you different?"

"Because I'm a different age from Ami and Noam."

"That's true. Is there anything else different about you?"

Suddenly, the whole idea of being different seems intriguing to Ezra— and much more appealing than the siblings traveling in a tree house to meet Abraham Lincoln. He has discovered some version of himself in a book—and now he seems more motivated to read. Instead of forcing books on him, Shawn follows his lead and finds books on the theme of feeling different. She doesn't worry about grade level or difficulty. She wants Ezra to find himself in the books—to discover stories that reflect his own experience.

He reads about Elmer, an elephant with a multicolored, patchwork hide who tries to fit in with the herd of gray elephants, then is finally celebrated for his uniqueness. He reads about Curious George, the little monkey whose inquisitiveness (not to mention his inability to consider the consequences of his actions) leads him on unexpected adventures and lands him in trouble again and again. He reads about Ferdinand, the bull who opts to lie in a field, smelling flowers while the other bulls dream of fighting a matador; and about Stellaluna, a fruit bat trying to fit in with a nest of birds. As they read the books, Shawn doesn't pester Ezra with questions about what he's picturing. She knows that part of what he sees as he reads about these misfits who never quite blend in with the group is himself.

Over time Ezra's magnetic attraction to books only increases, as he uses his animal encyclopedias and his growing collection of books about animation to accumulate storehouses of data. It's clear that he can read and absorb fairly sophisticated information about mammals or *Star Wars* or *The Simpsons*. What is difficult to know is whether he has developed the ability to read an ordinary story. Or perhaps the real problem is simply that he hasn't figured out how to communicate to others what he perceives.

It's a chilly April morning when Ezra is eleven, several years after his seven months of homeschooling with his mother. Shawn and I visit his school for a conference with his sixth-grade instructor. When Shawn asks Ms. Williams—young, reserved—how Ezra is doing in English, she shrugs and then describes how, in reading group, he reads aloud with great expression and fluency.

"And does he know what he's reading?" Shawn asks.

Ms. Williams shrugs again and says nothing. Then she pulls out a manila folder and shows us a series of reading quizzes.

"It's hard to tell," she finally says.

Shawn and I flip through the loose pages, most riddled with question marks Ezra has penciled in after questions. On some pages he has sketched Bart Simpson or SpongeBob. Elsewhere he has penciled in cartoons of giraffes and lions.

"If he's understanding," the teacher says, "it doesn't show up on the tests."

Several months after that, it's a Friday evening, near the end of a lengthy dinner our family has shared with Shawn's parents, Del and Sandey. Most of the family—Shawn, the other boys, and her father—have left our dining room to stretch out in the family room. Ezra lingers at the table, lured by a Tofutti Cutie and some grapes—to sit with his grandmother and me. We are trying to ask him about his week in school, and he avoids the question—as usual—but then says something I don't quite hear.

"Did you say 'Amelia Earhart'?" I ask.

"Yeah, Amelia Earhart," he says. "First woman of flight."

"How do you know about Amelia Earhart?" I ask.

"Amelia Earhart flew around the world," Ezra says.

"She did."

"Yeah, and her navigator was Fred Noonan."

I listen.

"Then her plane went down near Howland Island in the Pacific Ocean, yeah," he continues.

"Where did you hear about that?" Sandey asks.

"That was in 'First Lady of Flight,'" he says.

"Where was—"

"That was the first story in the theme 'What Really Happened?'" He's talking about the reading textbook his class has been reading all year— the one the teacher wasn't sure he understood. Before I can ask him anything else, Ezra keeps talking. "And then the story 'Passage to Freedom.' That was in the theme 'Courage.'" He begins detailing the characters in the story about Mr. Sugihara, a Japanese diplomat who saved Polish Jews during the Holocaust.

Sandey and I listen to Ezra, a smile on his face, review aloud the details of every story his sixth-grade class has read—the title, the characters, which section of the textbook contains which stories. He has been reading all along. I think of how Ms. Williams shrugged in the conference, how she told us she simply didn't know how much Ezra understood. I think of the test sheets with the blank spaces and the scrawled question marks and doodled cartoons. All this time, Ezra has been taking it all in—the characters, the stories, the themes, and the details. He just didn't know how to show that—or, more likely, just didn't feel like it. I wonder how much my son has been stowing away without being able to share what he was absorbing. I pause to ponder what potential Ezra has that he has been keeping hidden all this time.

And I think of that afternoon many years earlier, when Ezra sat on the floor paging through a book that Elana told us he was reading. I am beginning to think she was right.

CHAPTER SEVEN

Gumby, Cheerios, and Red T-shirts

I'm walking with Ezra in Westwood—though if I had thought the plan through even a tiny bit more, I probably wouldn't be doing this at all. It's a warm spring evening. Ezra is eight, and we're on our way to a store called Aahs!!, a gift shop near the UCLA campus. The store's name sounds like "Oz," as in the Wizard, but it's spelled A-A-H-S, with two exclamation marks for emphasis. As in "oohs and aahs," indicating, perhaps, that it's a place one might find overwhelming, or where you might come to a realization.

For Ezra, it will be the former; for me, the latter.

Aahs!! is a gift shop in the way that Las Vegas is a town—a novelty store with psychedelic Day-Glo posters in the back and Halloween costumes year-round and shelves piled high with whoopee cushions. I should have known that for Ezra to encounter all of those doodads in one place might trigger disaster.

At this point, he has shown a not yet unhealthy fascination with *The*

Simpsons, a sharp contrast to the Nickelodeon and Disney fare he has generally favored. His interest was kindled by an old foot-tall plastic Bart Simpson among the wooden blocks and Beanie Babies crowding our playroom bins. Ezra started spotting that same face, with its bulging eyes and serrated flattop, around town on billboards, and then in a comic book we had bought for Ami. Passing notice has escalated to intrigue, fascination, and finally something like obsession. He has never viewed a single episode on TV, but the Simpsons—simple, bright, yellow, distinctive, ubiquitous— are natural objects for Ezra's attention. Day and night, he spouts information, data, and questions about Bart and his compadres.

This is the closest his taste has ever come to my own. I was a *Simpsons* fan from early on—partly because I had interviewed the show's creator in the program's first days, learning in the process that we had attended the same schools as children. This is a first: Not only is Ezra's taste veering toward what other eight-year-olds find appealing, but it is intersecting with my own. As a reward for good behavior, I have offered to take Ezra on a father-son shopping quest. The goal: procuring a small *Simpsons* toy.

"You can buy only one small thing," I keep reminding Ezra on the fifteen-minute drive. Oddly, despite a superhuman ability to remember birthdays and addresses, he can't seem to hang on to simple directives from his dad. I test him: "Can you get something *huge*?"

"*Noooo!*" he says from the backseat, drawing out the word.

"Are you going to run around the store?"

"*No!*" he promises.

"Who are you going to stay with?"

"Abba."

"What if you don't listen?"

"Then we have to leave."

"That's right."

I glance at Ezra in the rearview mirror and smile at how easily he is charmed. I envision driving him home as he delights over a five-dollar Bart Simpson pen, or maybe a key chain.

I park the Camry on a quiet side street. Ezra is running already.

I call after him: "Stop! Slow down!"

Trouble is, at eight years old, Ezra has not learned to slow down. He has only two speeds: fast and asleep. I grab his hand, clutching it as we wait at the crosswalk for the light to turn, then hold tight as we traverse the four lanes. From the sidewalk, Ezra can see into the Aahs!! windows, with their lively, brightly colored displays blending oversize cartoon characters with mannequins in frilly lingerie and novelty T-shirts. Excited, Ezra attempts to move even faster, and I struggle to slow him down, gripping his hand as we slip inside the store.

Aahs!! In seconds I know that this is the best and worst place possible for an eight-year-old boy who is easily overstimulated by the toy shelf at Walgreens. Every aisle is a cornucopia of schlock: pink coffee mugs with protruding breasts, snow globes and joy buzzers and fake vomit. Ezra notices none of that, breaking free of my grasp to speed toward the back of the store, where, just next to the cash register, he discovers his holy grail: an entire *Simpsons* island, a bulging, seven-foot-tall mountain of Simpsons. I watch my son quickly size up the display as if he has just happened upon a truckload of ice-cream sandwiches: Half of him is overcome with joy; half of him is paralyzed by the quandary of where to begin.

Before he takes another step, I kneel down at his level and firmly grab his shoulders.

"What did I say?" I ask. "What can you buy?"

Suddenly it's as if the conversation we shared in the car wasn't minutes ago but rather sometime in the Pleistocene era. He mumbles something, but keeps looking past me to the towering shelves of yellow curios. He is like a wild animal, surging with energy, operating on reflexes, impossible to harness.

"What are you allowed to buy?"

He keeps glancing away.

"Something *big*?" I ask.

"No."

"What are we getting?"

"Something small," he says evenly, quietly.

"Good," I say.

By then, though, it's too late. Amid the rubber action figures, the mugs, the T-shirts and chess sets, Ezra has spotted the object of his desire. His eyes—now as fully protruding as a Simpson's—are locked on the top shelf of the display. Pointing upward, Ezra begins to yell.

"The Homer!" he calls. "I want the *Homer*!"

I follow his focus to the tip-top shelf, zeroing in on the thing that has so captivated my son. It's yellow. It's bulging. It's bug-eyed. It's nearly as tall as Ezra himself. It's—

"The Homer! I want the *Homer*!"

"But that's not what we came—"

"I want the *Homer*!" he keeps shouting.

I quickly scan the shelves for something—*anything*—more within the allotted budget. A key chain? A comb? Feeling more anxious and sweatier by the second, I wave one knickknack after another in Ezra's face, trying to distract his gaze from the gigantic stuffed cartoon man. Ezra shakes his head and I anxiously search for more options.

"Ezra . . . *Look at me!*" I say, in what starts as a whisper but then emerges as a barely controlled holler. My sudden intensity and volume pique the attention of the surly woman behind the cash register, who glances up from a customer, peering over her reading glasses for just long enough to catch sight of an eight-year-old boy in shorts and a red T-shirt scampering up the shelves, hoisting his three-and-a-half-foot-tall body upward, one shelf at a time, higher and higher, closer and closer to the jackpot.

"Sir!" the cashier calls out. "You're going to have to control your—"

Before she can finish, I take hold of Ezra, who tries to wriggle from my grasp, his flailing limbs knocking over a rack of talking Krusty the Clown dolls. Flustered, I scramble to catch the merchandise and simultaneously catch my son's fall on the linoleum floor.

"But I *want* the Homer!" he keeps screaming. "I want the *Homer!*"

I feel every soul in the store glowering at us—the man waiting to pay for his exploding golf balls, the spiky-haired college kid scanning the greeting card aisle, the stock boy unpacking a box of windup chattering teeth. I feel flushed and sticky. I abandon all thoughts of persuading Ezra to settle for a more modest purchase.

"Abba, buy me the *Homer!*" he keeps calling, and I fear that my behavior is about to traverse the line of what constitutes acceptable parenting, even in a store that trades in fart candy and imitation vomit.

"That's it," I say. "We're going."

I grab his hand and tip my head to the right, gesturing toward the door. Ezra understands. I know this because he chooses this moment to render his body completely limp, and he falls from my grasp to the floor, folding himself into a fetal clutch on the cold floor.

"Don't make me *go!*" he cries, now wailing like the widows on TV news footage from the Middle East. Tears gush from his eyes; desperation fills his voice: "I waaaaant the *Hooooomer!*"

With the cashier and a gaggle of customers glaring, I yank Ezra by the arm, pulling him to his feet and then up the aisle, past the itchy toilet paper and the penis-shaped candles and out toward the door. Firmly and with conviction, I tug my son to the sidewalk outside, where he keeps turning around, sobbing wildly, begging to go back, pleading for the Homer. Trying to ignore his pleas, I keep yanking at his arm, but as we wait for the long crosswalk signal to change—it feels like a year passes as we wait by the curb—he rushes from my grip and, when I follow, takes hold of the corner of the building, sobbing and begging and clutching on so tight that his knuckles are turning white.

The sky is darkening, all kinds of people are walking by, and I'm trying to remember: *Why was it that I wanted to have children, again?* Did Shawn and I spend enough time researching this whole enterprise? It just seemed like the thing to do. Our parents had children; our grandparents raised kids. I guessed we should too. How hard could it be? What was the worst thing that could happen? I recall an expectation of clever banter over the family dinner table; I conjured images of playing catch with my kids on the lawn or driving them to piano lessons. I figured there would be rough moments, but I did not expect that fatherhood would entail moments like this, doing hand-to-hand-combat on the streets of Westwood, making desperate efforts to wrench eight-year-old knuckles from storefronts.

I am so focused on the work of prying flesh from stucco that I almost don't hear—

"Is that . . . Tom?"

I look up and find myself eye-to-eye with Jeff, the brother of a close friend, waving and trying to smile while also furrowing his brow in puzzlement, obviously trying to make sense of the tableau in front of him: a grown man trying to peel a third grader from a building.

"Anything I can help with?" Jeff says, haltingly.

I try to evince a smile. Ezra wails uncontrollably. I shake my head.

"Nah," I manage to say. "I think we're okay."

I should have listened to Ruth. The first professional we ever consulted about Ezra, the therapist offered some oblique advice a few short months into our sessions. Her morsel of wisdom seemed of little consequence back then, but it came to haunt me later.

"Very often, these kinds of children develop obsessions," Ruth said, "things they want to talk about exclusively all the time." She told us about one client, a girl from an ultraorthodox Jewish family, who had developed a severe and persistent preoccupation with Madonna. Not the mother of Jesus; that would have been trouble enough. *The* Madonna. The child ranted incessantly about Madonna's music and Madonna's boyfriends; she spewed detailed trivia about Madonna's songs, Madonna's videos, Madonna's wardrobe and Grammys. To teachers, playmates, anyone who would listen (and plenty of people who wouldn't), she would expound on Madonna. "And this," Ruth said, raising an eyebrow for emphasis, "was not a family in which that was okay."

I pondered that for a moment, conjuring a scene: of a long Sabbath table, candles aglow atop a white lace tablecloth, a zaftig matriarch at one end ladling matzo ball soup, her bearded, black-clad husband at the other, and ten or twelve children in between all paying rapt attention as little Rivka—pigtails, elbow-length sleeves, skirt to midcalf—holds forth about her favorite cuts from "Like a Virgin." Back when Ruth issued her warning, Ezra—then just three—hadn't settled on fixations beyond his plastic dinosaurs and jungle animals. In light of this new information, I imagined my little boy progressing up the evolutionary chain from stegosauruses to woolly mammoths to alligators, in a steady arc leading directly to pop divas. As I considered that, Ruth offered a cautionary thought. "Be careful what you expose him to," she said. "You don't know where it will lead."

I recall that ominous tidbit of advice on darkened Westwood Boulevard. Powerless to budge my shuddering, wailing bundle of tears, I'm now sitting cross-legged on the cool sidewalk, wondering how I might ever distract Ezra from what has become an all-consuming quest.

You don't know where it will lead, Ruth said.

Well, now I know.

In fact, I have recalled her words frequently in the months and years since, each time experiencing a discomfiting combination of anticipation and fear. *Be careful what you expose him to.* What will it be? What will Ezra fixate upon? In retrospect, those words of counsel have been among the least helpful bits of wisdom we have gathered in our journey with Ezra.

It drives me to books and articles and Web sites in search of information about children like Ezra, children with autism and Asperger's syndrome or children who are simply a bit odd. I keep coming across descriptions of little boys who are unable to function among peers, and who develop unusual preoccupations with sets of trivia—commuter train schedules, say, or insect species. I read repeatedly about a boy in England with exhaustive command of the minutiae of refrigerator fans and motors. I am confident Ezra will not find his way to train schedules. For kids in West Los Angeles, public transportation is about as remote and abstract as molecular theory. Refrigerator motors? He is certainly obsessed with the *contents* of our refrigerator, but I don't think he is even conscious of the mechanical gizmos keeping his snack food chilled.

Be careful what you expose him to.

How, I sometimes wonder, will we do that? Could those boys' mothers and fathers have avoided exposing their tykes to trains, or insects, or refrigerators? Could dangerous, life-sucking obsessions be lurking around every corner? Sometimes I watch Ezra take in the world and wonder what he might seize upon next.

Should we have kept him from watching *Sesame Street*? As a toddler, Ezra sat mesmerized just like millions of other children, idly picking at his Cheerios as he took in Bert and Ernie's latest tiff. And then, at a moment that escaped our notice, he crossed over into a different zone. He was no longer just another toddler hooked on PBS; he was positively addicted to the Muppets. He spent long hours paging through picture books, viewing and reviewing drawings of Cookie Monster and Grover and Zoe. His wasn't mere enthusiasm. Addiction was closer to what it was—and not just to watching the television show, but to populating his world with these characters, to the exclusion of human beings and real interactions. That is the behavior that shows up in Karen's preschool classroom, where Ezra seems lost and drifting, except when he spots pictures of the characters he knows from *Sesame Street*.

Ezra's fixations are powerful and all-consuming, but not endless. In time, he turns his focus from Elmo to another imaginary character: Thomas the Tank Engine, the quirky anthropomorphic locomotive who had his own PBS program, populated by a mixed multitude of stiffly animated train cars, a helicopter, a bus, and a handful of odd humans.

At four, Ezra chatters nonstop about Thomas and Thomas's friends, holding forth on the topic to the exclusion of almost anything else. When I mention this to other parents, some smile empathetically and assure me that, well, that's just how kids are at that age—and tell me how their little ones are just as absorbed with the objects of their own infatuation: Pokémon, say, or baseball cards, or Barbie.

"I know just what you mean," they say.

I know they don't. I suppose these mothers and fathers are trying to be reassuring. Instead, I take it as myopic. When one mom insists that her son, too, prattles on about Thomas "all day long," I know she is being hyperbolic. I'm not. For a while, every time Ezra speaks, it is to say something about Thomas—a phrase or a question or a description. When he wakes up in the morning ("Is Percy friendly?"), when I step in the door in the evening after work ("Diesel is grumpy!"), when he is in the bath ("James is going very fast"), over pizza dinner ("Thomas is a really useful engine"), when we are settling him down to bed ("Henry is very long"), he keeps the chatter going.

It began innocently enough, when he received a gift of a single two-inch-long wooden Thomas figure. I rarely see him actually play with the train. Rather, he carries it around the house, sometimes holding it close to his face, intently examining its details. He shows more interest in the sheet that came folded inside the plastic box, a roster with photos and descriptions of half a dozen other train characters. He carefully guards the sheet, and before long knows each character, identifying it by its distinctive coloring and unique facial features.

Soon, we buy him a second character, and Ezra does the same thing: closely scrutinizes it, puts it away in a box, and then carefully studies the sheet of other trains. In time, I watch his passing interest transform into passion and then infatuation, until giving Ezra a cute wooden train is like handing a crack pipe to an addict. The more Thomas he has, the more he craves. Something about the tactile sensation of holding these characters in his hands, or something about owning them—simply having them in his possession—seems to give Ezra an emotional lift. He shows so little awareness of other children—or anything else—that Shawn and I are happy to see him interested in something that other four-year-olds like. So we feed his habit, one train car at a time.

I realize that the Thomas fervor has gotten the best of me, too, the afternoon I pick Ezra up at preschool and drive him to a model-train specialty store housed in a building that is a replica of Los Angeles's train station. By the time I notice the sign just inside the door warning parents to watch young children—or pay for damage—Ezra has dashed ahead of me, displaying not a trace of interest in the aisles of train equipment and the intricate, minutely detailed scale models of villages and cities. He keeps running until he finds what he is hunting for: a toddler-size table with an elaborate Thomas display featuring dozens of his beloved characters arrayed on endless curves of interlocking wooden tracks, on bridges, in train sheds.

"Thomas!" he cries with glee.

"You like Thomas?" asks a salesman, who appears out of nowhere. Before I can stop him, he has produced a chunky blue box, holding it out for Ezra to see. "Have you seen the Mountain Tunnel Set?" he asks. "Sixty pieces, two engines, the helicopter, you get a bridge . . ."

"Not today, thanks," I say, trying to distract Ezra's attention from the hundred-and-forty-dollar kit and back to the table with its tracks.

Too late.

For days and weeks, our family lives with Ezra's newest fixation: the

Mountain Tunnel Set. It becomes a mantra. "I want the Mountain Tunnel Set," he repeats day and night. "But I *love* the Mountain Tunnel Set. I *neeeeed* the Mountain Tunnel Set." I begin to understand how prisoners of war can be worn into submission through the mere process of repetition.

I suggest that he make it a birthday request, hoping that might put a stop to his incessant begging. Instead, it causes a new obsession: He begins compulsively counting the days to his fifth birthday. At least, I figure, that period will end when his birthday arrives. It is a few weeks away, but I can live with that. As the day nears, I imagine Ezra's happiness at finally realizing his dream, smiling to myself as I picture him playing with his brothers on the playroom floor, guiding the little wooden trains over the tracks and through the tunnels.

When the day comes, Ezra awakens in the predawn hours, stumbles from his bed, and appears at our doorway in his blue dinosaur-print pajamas, then dashes to the living room and discovers a box half his size wrapped in the Sunday comics. Tearing it open, he squeals with happiness.

"The Mountain Tunnel Set! *It's the Mountain Tunnel Set!*"

I smile at Shawn as we watch him peel away the wrapping paper, feeling a surge of happiness at seeing such joy in our son—such spontaneous elation in a boy who so often seems uncomfortable and discontent. I kneel down to help him open the box and set up the tracks. Ezra shows scarcely any interest in arranging the wooden train tracks. Instead, he takes out the train car characters that came in the box (and a few others we have thrown in), lines them up in a row, saying each of their names as he places them on the hardwood floor, and then begins perusing the back of the carton, looking at pictures of other Thomas sets. He's not going to *play* with the set—at least, not the way that most kids do, creating imaginary adventures for the little engines. Having this set only seems to make him crave more: more bite-size wooden engines; more predictable characters that fall into neat categories—friendly, grumpy, young, old; more contrived facial expressions. *People* can fill Ezra with anxiety. Little wooden trains calm him down.

Each obsession arrives mysteriously and unannounced, like a phantom that sneaks into our home in the night and seizes my son, snatching his focus. I cannot predict when one will depart and another will arrive. Nor can I ever imagine what might catch his attention next.

After Thomas comes Gumby. *Gumby*, the bendable green clay man. We are visiting the home of one of Ami's best friends when Ezra sneaks away to explore on his own, and emerges from one of the bedrooms holding a flexible Gumby figure he has stumbled upon. None of the children seems particularly attached to the toy, so the parents suggest that Ezra take it home. It quickly becomes his constant companion. He carries it with him to school, to the park, to the supermarket, and to bed.

Unlike Thomas, Gumby is unheard-of among the preschool set. To them, Gumby is practically extinct, a toy that has gone the way of record players and Lincoln Logs. Ezra doesn't care (or notice) that his peers are taken with Game Boy and Yu-Gi-Oh! Ezra likes Gumby. Something about the simple body, the bright color, the fixed smile, and the friendly eyes appeals to him, and he wants more.

I search on eBay, placing bids of a dollar or two on two-inch rubber figurines that anonymous strangers are discarding from their garages: Pokey, Gumby's orange horse sidekick; a pair of red bad guys called the Blockheads; and Goo, a blue, yellow-haired, bloblike mermaid. Ezra celebrates each new arrival. Late at night, in the glow of the computer monitor and in the midst of bidding wars over hunks of rubber, I occasionally pause to wonder why I am doing this—why I am helping my son to pursue his eccentric interests. Other boys Ezra's age are trading Pokémon cards or are starting to play soccer and learn karate. When Ezra pulls out his Gumby collection, they just stare, as if he has pulled liverwurst from his lunch pail. As Ezra accumulates characters and videos and builds a mental storehouse of Gumby's animated adventures, he is doing so entirely alone.

Of course, Ezra doesn't even realize how isolated he is. One Saturday afternoon, I am walking in the neighborhood with him when we cross paths with a doctor we know.

"Say hello to Dr. Becker," I whisper to Ezra as we approach.

He smiles. "Hello, Dr. Becker!" he says with enthusiasm. "Do you know about Gumby?"

The man just looks puzzled.

It isn't difficult to see what captures Ezra's focus and brings him comfort. His sensory wiring makes normal sensations painful: He covers his ears at sudden noises and seems agonized by eye contact. Gumby doesn't change much, barely moves, and asks nothing of him. It is Ezra's small effort to exert some control, to make his world easier to take.

That might also explain the red period. For two years of his life, Ezra insists on wearing only red clothing: red tops, maroon sweatpants, bright red Stride Rites. He has a red fleece jacket and a red backpack and red sweatshirts. It starts with shirts—in particular, a red T-shirt he began to favor around age four. After a while he insists on that shirt exclusively. If Shawn or I try slipping another one over his head, he wriggles out of it, shouting, "Red shirt! Red shirt!" We buy him a half dozen red shirts. On days at the end of the family laundry cycle, when the red items are scarce, he wails and squirms and tosses clothing across the room.

Anytime he has a choice of color—crayons, felt markers, bedsheets, baseball caps—he chooses red. He insists on Red Delicious apples, ripe red tomatoes, Hawaiian Punch Slurpees at 7-Eleven, cherry Popsicles at the park. He methodically sifts through the Froot Loops like an archaeologist searching for treasure to separate out the red ones. He favors red characters in movies and TV shows—Lightning McQueen, the race car in *Cars*, Bob the Tomato in *Veggie Tales*, the entire family from the Pixar movie *The Incredibles*. He literally leaps with excitement when fire engines race by. Not because of the sirens and lights; he is simply thrilled to see so much bright red paint all in one place.

The red phase has its advantages. It is easy to shop for him, less stressful choosing his clothes in the morning, and when he wanders away from us and the other boys—as he so often does—at the supermarket or the park, we have only to search for the red blur streaking past.

Why red? I sometimes ask him. Ezra never has a reason. He just likes red. Press him more and he says: "It's a bright color." Ezra doesn't like surprises, resists change, and craves sameness.

Yet his obsessions change unpredictably and mysteriously, coming and going like seasonal influenza viruses or diet fads. I can never discern why he grabs onto a particular fixation, can never predict when he will abruptly drop it, and can never imagine what he might seize upon next. Mysteriously, Thomas gives way to Gumby, Gumby to *Veggie Tales*, *The Simpsons*, and *Star Wars*, *Star Wars* to geography. For a while around age seven, he obsessively draws maps of the entire Western United States from memory, neatly fitting Montana into Idaho, precisely interlocking the panhandles of Oklahoma and Texas, producing detailed hand drawings with remarkable recall over and over and over.

Then come breakfast cereals. It isn't so much about eating them. Ezra talks about Cheerios and Cap'n Crunch, reads their boxes, commits their ingredients to memory, yammers about their mascots, and launches into discourses about cereal taxonomy, drawing elaborate family trees of the Kellogg, General Mills, and Post clans. Toucan Sam—the Froot Loops spokesbird—and the Trix rabbit feel larger than life to him. He treats the nutritional panel on Rice Krispies and Life like sacred texts, reciting calorie counts and grams of sugar per serving like holy mantras.

Visiting the homes of friends or relatives, Ezra blurts out a question to the first person he encounters: "What kind of cereal do you have here?"

Usually he is met by stunned silence, as the host tries to make sure she has heard correctly. "Cereal?" she says. "Oh, can I get you a snack?" By then, Ezra has scurried past and found his way, uninvited, to the kitchen, where he is rapidly opening and shutting one cupboard after another, quickly scanning in single-minded pursuit of Cocoa Krispies.

"You want a cookie, sweetie?" the hostess will say. "How about some yogurt?" The first couple of times this happens, I am as mystified as anyone. I feel alternately chagrined at his behavior and frustrated that I can't figure out how to turn off whatever it is that compels it. I understand that it has little to do with eating cereal. Ezra simply feels a need to see what products are there. Being in a house without knowing what cardboard boxes lurk in the cupboards fills him with an intolerable anxiety. That knowledge makes his world more complete. Weeks or months later he will spot adult acquaintances at the library or in the drugstore and recollect their breakfast choices with perfect recall.

"Hi, Bonnie," he says. "Do you still have Post Honeycombs?"

Those encounters leave people both stupefied and charmed. And so am I. As Ezra grows and develops, I live with a juxtaposition of feelings: concern about what might capture his fancy next and fascination and pride in my son's ability to master a topic and use it to engage with other people. Even if that subject is breakfast food.

I do understand the instinct so many parents have to fight battles, trying to nudge children toward more mainstream pursuits. I gauge our other sons' progress by the kinds of standard measurements most mothers and fathers use: We have watched Ami's evolution through the ever-larger trophies he collects at the end of each baseball and soccer season, a series of student government positions, and friendships; Noam rises through the ranks at the karate studio, each new belt and patch marking another level of accomplishment, and makes his way through the Suzuki violin book, showing ever-increasing ability and focus. Tracking Ezra's advancement is different. With each passing month and year, he grows more singular.

At some point I realize that is precisely the way to build a relationship with my son: through the trains, the Gumby figures, the endless trail of red. Instead of seeing his obsessions as traits to change, Shawn and I come to view them as opportunities to build a bond—a quirky, unpredictable, whimsical bond, to be sure, but a strong one. Instead of lamenting that we can't have an ordinary conversation with our son about the Dodgers or sitcoms or what happened in school that day, we join him. We follow his lead.

Sometimes that brings me to unexpected places. I find myself sending my hard-earned dollars via PayPal to a guy in Missouri selling decades-old clay-animated characters, or standing in line at the Target store, my shopping cart filled with red jerseys and pajamas. Sometimes I pause and wonder whether we are doing the right thing.

Over time, though, I come to realize a reward: Ezra understands that another human cares about what he cares about. Slowly, over time, our connection grows, and so does his potential to have other relationships with people, friendships based on something more than Gumby.

That is why it is worth enduring what comes to be known in our family as the Homer incident—that awful outing to the Aahs!! store, an adventure that concludes when I finally drag him, sobbing and wailing, across Westwood Boulevard and back to the car. "I just wanted the *Homer*!" he keeps crying, his face distorted in exaggerated pain, his hands clenched with tension and pleading.

"I know, sweetie," I tell him, trying to calm him down. "I know it's hard."

He cries all through the fifteen-minute drive home, and then runs from the backseat of the car across the lawn and into the house, slipping silently into the bedroom he shares with his brothers.

After a few minutes, I go in and find him in his top bunk, the covers stretched over his head. When I pull them off, his eyes are red from the sobbing.

"I wanted the Homer so *bad*," Ezra says.

"I know," I say. "Sometimes you don't get what you want."

That evening, I offer Ezra a way for him to earn the Homer doll he wants so dearly. I draw up a chart with twenty-eight boxes and tell him that if he can control his behavior and avoid those kinds of tantrums for four weeks—and curtail the begging—then maybe we can venture back to Aahs!!

"I can get the Homer?" he asks, brightening for the first time all evening.

"If you're good." I point to the chart in my hand. "Can you be good for four weeks?"

"I can be good."

"No talking about the Homer?"

"I will be good," he says, and, in seconds, he stops crying. His entire countenance changes, as if a demon that has been possessing him has fled, leaving the same gentle, sweet boy who accompanied me to the store a few hours earlier. Then, in a calm, singsong voice, less ecstatic than relieved: "I can get the Homer."

Every evening that month, when I get home from work, Ezra excitedly reports to me that he has had a good day. Whenever he starts asking for the doll, I raise a finger or an eyebrow in warning—and he stops.

Four weeks after the disaster, the two of us pile into the car and drive back to the Aahs!! store. Together, we walk into the store. Together, we stroll to the *Simpsons* display. I reach up and grab the doll for him, and hand my charge card to the surly woman behind the register, who, I am thankful, doesn't seem to recognize us. We walk out into a warm Los Angeles evening, I clutch Ezra's hand, and he hugs his new two-and-a-half-foot-tall yellow doll.

"I got the Homer," he says, matter-of-factly.

"Yep," I say. "You got the Homer."

CHAPTER EIGHT

Typing Lessons

When Ezra is six years old, my editor at the magazine calls with an intriguing assignment. He wants me to interview a boy who cannot speak. Tito Mukhopadhyay has made international headlines for an extraordinary ability: Though his severe autism renders him unable to utter a meaningful sentence, he is composing sublime poetry that reveals a complex and unusual intellect. Tito and his mother are visiting Los Angeles from their home in Bangalore, India, so that scientists can benefit from his unparalleled ability to explain the workings of his mind.

I have covered scores of heartrending human-interest stories for the magazine. This one is different. This time I bring my own questions.

I feel excited and curious as I arrive on a warm December afternoon at the white stucco apartment building just off Hollywood Boulevard. Only a few blocks from the tourist bustle of Grauman's Chinese Theatre and the Hollywood Walk of Fame, it seems an odd home—even temporarily—for a boy from a small flat halfway across the world. Tito's mother greets me.

Soma is in her early forties, tiny and self-assured. She introduces me to Tito, fourteen and in the midst of an adolescent growth spurt. He is a bundle of tremors and paroxysms, in constant motion and with eyes that seem permanently locked in a far-off gaze. Immediately I recognize shades of Ezra. Tito does not speak, except for some occasional phrases, almost whispered.

While Tito paces the small living room, gazing at his hands fluttering in front of his face, I interview Soma. She tells me how she ignored doctors' early warnings that Tito would never be able to communicate in a meaningful way. She watched Tito stare intently at a calendar, clearly focused on understanding it. Then she taught him how to count and to read the letters of the alphabet on a paper chart. She read him one of Aesop's fables when he was three, then asked him what it was about. He pointed to the letters on the chart: C-R-O-W.

"Once it started," she says, "there was no limit."

Instead of giving up on him, she began reading to her son from classics—Dickens, Hardy, and Shakespeare—confident that, although his body showed almost no outward sign, his mind was taking it all in.

I think about all of the times I have watched Ezra's eyes and wondered what he is thinking, what he was feeling, what he understands. I envy Soma's maternal instinct and consider the pure faith that must have driven her. I try to imagine what must have gone through her mind as she sat in her Bangalore home and turned pages, day after day, reading *A Tale of Two Cities* to her mute little boy as his body rocked and convulsed and his eyes stared off into the distance.

Soma tells me how she taught her young son to write, first fastening a pencil to his right hand with elastic bands and slowly guiding him as he traced the alphabet on paper. Over months and years, the boy scratched out one letter at a time in broad, uneven strokes as his mother sat by his side offering encouragement. In time, he was writing poetry—about trees, trains, and how he experiences life.

"May I ask Tito some questions?" I ask Soma.

She prompts her son to sit. He settles beside me on a couch. I hand him a legal pad and a pencil. Soma sits on his other side, issuing verbal prompts—"Go ahead! . . . Next, please!" The combination of his flailing body and distant look give a sense of a kind of wild, untamed energy; the apartment can barely contain him. When he begins writing, he reveals himself as refined, clever, and sophisticated. Though I am a quarter century his senior, I feel like I am drinking in wisdom from an older, wiser soul.

I ask why he moves around so much. He explains that he cannot feel his body unless it is in motion. Best of all for him, he says, is being submerged in water. I think of Ezra, who thrives in the bathtub, who opens up and communicates in swimming pools in ways we have not seen anywhere else.

I ask about eye contact, and Tito tells me that his brain is incapable of using more than one sense at once. "I can either see or hear," he writes. "I cannot do both at the same time."

In the midst of the interview, Tito stands up without warning and walks across the room. Soma tries to guide him back, saying, "Sit, sit!" and firmly nudging him, but he moves toward an open window, apparently drawn by a gentle wind sweeping into the apartment. He looks upward and smiles, the way golden retrievers delight in catching a breeze in a moving car.

When he returns to the sofa, I tell him about Ezra. I ask him to explain why my son is constantly asking lately whether faces he sees are happy or sad.

"He's stimming on the question," Tito writes. *Stimming*. In autism circles, it's shorthand for self-stimulating behavior—repetitive movements that somehow prove arousing. I have never thought of Ezra's incessant questions this way.

"You mean he knows the answer," I say, "but it makes him feel good to ask?"

"Yes," he writes.

I have more questions, but Tito, then thirty minutes into the interview, can no longer sit still for long enough to keep writing. He's asking Soma for dinner, and he doesn't have the focus to continue. His mother beckons him back, but then apologizes. I assure her it's fine.

Leaving the building, I walk up Hollywood Boulevard, clutching the pad with Tito's writing. The pages are much more than the notes I will need to write my article. I feel like I'm carrying something sacred.

Part of what makes the papers so precious is the promise they hold for Shawn and for me. I have long believed that Ezra has more thoughts than he is able to communicate. I understand that his habit of verbal dumping conceals what Ezra carries deep inside: a lucid mind, an eager soul, a yearning to connect. As he repeats his *Winnie the Pooh* line for the hundredth time, I have looked into his eyes, certain that something else is going on in his mind. Part of me feels disappointed that I couldn't ask Tito more questions about Ezra, but I also realize that another boy, no matter how brilliant, cannot explain my son to me any more than doctors or therapists or books can. I will need to find my way in, just as Soma did.

When I get home, Shawn and the boys are waiting for me for dinner. Four of us sit down, and Ezra leaves his chair empty, as usual, moving about the house, flapping his arms, and entertaining himself. *Stimming*. As I look at him, I don't see the six-year-old boy, but try to imagine him at

Tito's age, a young man entering adolescence. I wonder: When Ezra turns thirteen or fourteen, what parts of himself might he be able to share?

I ponder the irony that Tito cannot speak, but can be so articulate, while Ezra can talk easily, but so much of what he says is . . . stimming. I wonder, if I could get him to sit for long enough to write or type, what profound worlds might my son reveal? While Ezra has been watching Disney videos and *Bear in the Big Blue House,* should we have been reading him Shakespeare? Have I already failed him by not undertaking the kinds of heroic, selfless measures Soma has?

On the other hand, it is difficult to imagine eliciting a written conversation with Ezra. For one thing, he has trouble with the physical mechanics of writing, experiencing such difficulty with fine motor coordination that an occupational therapist intervened to help him learn to write his letters. For neurological reasons I don't fully grasp, he has particular trouble with letters like S and Z, with diagonal strokes, so when he writes his name, he tilts the second letter, making the middle stroke vertical. Writing seems almost painful to him.

And he is so peripatetic that I hardly have the opportunity to sit down and try. Ezra at six is a constant blur. Like a shark, he is unable to live without constant motion.

From the dinner table, I watch my son slip into a fit of laughter at something only he understands. I think about Tito rushing to the window, savoring the breeze and writing in rhyme, and I wonder if Ezra will ever share in words the things that make him smile and giggle.

It's two years later, a Sunday. Ezra, now eight, is stuck, as he so often seems to be. He has trapped himself in a verbal loop, fixating on his latest Disney obsession, *Snow White and the Seven Dwarfs.* He is riveted by these seven little men—each with a distinctive face, a fixed set of expressions, each with a name that sums up his personality and disposition. They have everything Ezra is drawn to: categories, predictable personalities, bright colors. He has frequently returned from school recently with a backpack full of drawings he has etched with crayons on lined notebook paper, his own renditions of Sneezy and Happy, Dopey and Doc. The pictures are rough but remarkably detailed, showing Doc's spectacles, Sleepy's droopy eyelids and robe.

Now he wants more. Somehow he has convinced himself that he desperately needs to get to the Disney Store in search of some kind of figurine versions of the dwarfs. And he won't let go.

"We *will* go to the Disney Store at Westside Pavilion," he tells me.

"No, Ez."

"We will. Say yes, Abba. We *will* go."

I shake my head, but Ezra is undeterred, repeating his request with increasing urgency. The more firmly I refuse his demand, the more energetic his entreaties become. *Yes, we will, yes-we-will, yeswewill.* He is stimming on the words. He is also determined, pushing his face into mine, struggling to find any way to convince his father to give in.

"Yes, Abba. We *will* go to the Disney Store today. You *will* take me."

I shake my head, trying to ignore him.

"But we *must* go."

I feel both exasperated and fascinated by his persistence.

I hold steady, trying to look stern. We are locked in a standoff. Neither of us is budging. And then I get an idea: Maybe this is the moment I can induce Ezra to express himself in writing. In recent months, he has begun showing interest in the desktop computer we keep in an armoire in the living room. Since he has discovered that he can use Google to search for images, I have watched him sit at the keyboard, using a single index finger to type in the names of one animal after another: pigs, cows, bears, sheep. Mesmerized, he clicks on the mouse and stares at the monitor, surveying screen after screen of photos. But will he type more than the few letters of an animal's name?

I motion for Ezra to come with me to the computer. I sit on the black desk chair, pulling up a folding chair for Ezra. He sits, but bounces and squirms, a bundle of anxious, uncontainable energy. Without speaking, I type one sentence:

"Ezra will write here what he wants to tell Abba."

"But you *need* to take me," he says aloud, still begging for the Disney Store.

Silently, I point at the words on the monitor. I wait for him to read them, and wonder whether he will slow down and focus for long enough to internalize them, and whether, if he does, there is any chance that Ezra will respond in kind.

Should I read the words to him? I wonder. Will that grab his attention? I tap my right index finger on the monitor, where the first word appears: *Ezra.*

He leans forward in his chair, reading.

"But I want to . . ."

I hold a finger to my lips: *Shhhh.* I point to the screen again, thinking: *Should I tell him what to do?* When he looks like he is about to plead again, I hold the finger to his lips and shake my head again—*no*—letting the silence do its work. I extend my left hand, tapping lightly on the keyboard, then touch the monitor again with my index finger.

This will never work, I think. *He's just not ready.* I am about to concede and let Ezra escape. And then Ezra sits up, reaches out for the keyboard, and, using only his right index finger, begins pressing on the keys.

"I . . . w-i-l-l . . ."

He looks at the monitor to make sure the words are appearing. Reassured, he looks back to the keyboard and keeps typing:

"I . . . will . . . go . . . to . . . the . . . Disney . . . Store . . . with . . . Abba."

When he finishes, he looks up at me, eyes serious, then pleading. He nods vigorously, first his head, then practically his whole upper body. I can't help but smile. They are the same nine words that he has been repeating for the previous eight hours. But now they feel different. Ezra has communicated in an entirely new way. To me it feels like the famous scene in *The Miracle Worker,* when Annie Sullivan pumps water into Helen Keller's hands while spelling the word, and Helen makes the connection: "W-a-t-e-r . . . Water! Water!"

I will go to the Disney Store with Abba. The moment feels pregnant with possibility.

I grab the keyboard and quickly tap out my response:

"What will you do there?"

Ezra, still silent, leans forward again and reads my message. Without hesitating, he punches the keys with his index finger, typing his response:

"I will not act like a two-year-old."

"That's good. But what WILL you do, Ezra?"

"I will lisen."

"You will listen to who?"

"To abba."

"Why do you want to go to the Disney Store?"

"Because I like the Disney Store."

"What do you want to do there?"

"I want witch snow white and the seven dwarfs thing there is."

I call to mind an afternoon some years earlier, when Ezra was four. At that age, most children are nonstop squawk boxes, bursting with questions and opinions, exploring the world, learning right from wrong. Ezra at four was so detached that he often seemed not to register when someone spoke to him. His hearing was fine, and he was not being defiant; it simply didn't occur to Ezra to respond. We would call to him—at mealtime, or to get in the car for school, or when we simply couldn't find him—and hear only silence.

Then on that one afternoon I called to him: *"Ezzzraaaaaa!"*

After a second, emanating from the backyard, I heard his high-pitched reply: *"Whaaaaaat?"*

Shocked, I ran to get Shawn from another room.

"Did you hear that?" I asked.

"What?" she asked.

"I called Ezra and he answered."

I tried again. Again, he answered from the backyard. We savored the moment the way other parents celebrate a baby's first steps. Our son was responding.

That was what passed for a breakthrough when Ezra was four.

And now this. Our prosaic, typed exchange about the Disney Store is, in fact, the longest continuous conversation I have ever had with my eight-year-old son. I have the instinct to hold his arm and keep him in the chair, because I keep worrying that Ezra is about to bolt, fleeing my presence as he has so many times over the years.

Remarkably, he does not flee. Ezra calmly and carefully reads each sentence and phrase I type, giving it a moment's thought, and then pecking out his response with deliberation and silent confidence. He scarcely wavers from his agenda: We're going to the Disney Store. Now, though, instead of repeating the same phrase over and over, he tries every angle into the issue.

"How will you feel if I tell you that you cannot buy anything today?"

"I will not cry."

"What will you do?"

"I will be good."

"I like to be with you all the time but when you are in stores and you ask to buy LOTS OF THINGS I get upset. It makes me sad."

"I will get anything I want."

"No. You will not! We can look, but we cannot buy toys today."

"Yes we can buy toys today."

"Do you have money?"

"No. I do not."

"Then how can you buy toys?"

"You can get money at the bank."

"No. The bank is closed on Sunday."

"You can get money today."

Ezra is not stuck repeating the same words. He also isn't a pushover. My furtive dream has been that if I could ever get Ezra to type he might, like Tito, reveal some deep, hidden side of himself. Instead, the remarkable breakthrough in this conversation is that he is participating at all. And the written version of Ezra is strikingly similar to the spoken version. He is himself, only more so. He uses the same quirky syntax. *I want witch snow white and the seven dwarfs thing there is.* That is the way Ezra talks at age eight, creating his own unique grammar, probably because that is the way his brain processes the words he hears others speak.

While I have his attention, I decide to probe a bit:

"Ezra, can I ask you a question? What makes you feel happy?"

"When you let me go to the Disney Store today."

"But what else makes you happy?"

"When you say: 'Yes!'"

"When I say 'Yes' to what?"

"To let me go to the Disney Store today."

He isn't trying to be funny or clever. It is the only way Ezra knows how to be when he wants something—persistent, single-minded, inflexible, intent. Perhaps it is his determination that is keeping him in this dialogue. That's fine with me. I try a few other questions to see if Ezra will open up a bit.

"Who's your favorite person to be with?"

"Abba."

"Why?"

"Because you're my dad."

"Are you different from Ami?"

"Yes."

"What makes you different?"

"I want to be in Ami's class."

"Why?"

"Because I do."

By then, Ezra is squirming again in his chair, taking a bit longer to grab the keyboard, and assuming the more familiar flight mode. I look at my watch. We have been passing the keyboard back and forth for nearly an hour, with barely a spoken word between us, except for my occasional prompts—"keep going," "just a little more"—to keep his attention on the screen. Ezra isn't writing soul-searching poetry or revealing a deep understanding of life he has previously concealed. (But he has convinced me to take him to the Disney Store—where, alas, he is disappointed to find no dwarf toys.)

Ezra in type is just Ezra.

If some part of me feels disappointed, the greater part finds it comforting, even exciting. I have spent nearly an hour in conversation with the same boy who has eluded me for years. And maybe he wasn't hiding anything after all.

CHAPTER NINE

I Just Know

At first I think we're experiencing an earthquake. I'm lying in bed when I feel the house shake—*thud, thud, thud*—and then I hear a voice shouting something I can't quite make out. It's coming from just outside our bedroom. I sit up and listen more carefully. Somebody's jumping up and down. It's Ezra.

"It's February first!" he is saying with the kind of enthusiasm most people reserve for overtime soccer goals and airport greetings. "It's February *fiiiirrrrst!*" I'm not sure what the significance of that is. I scramble out of bed and into the hallway, where eight-year-old Ezra, still in pajamas, is pacing in small circles on the carpet, looking at nothing in particular. As he does most days, he has risen at full speed. Early morning grogginess is a foreign concept.

"It's *February first*, Abba!" he says to me with so much gusto that the words roll out like a cheer.

"What's happening on February first?" I ask, still not quite awake.

"It's the first day of the new month!" he says, and he keeps running and shouting.

That's it. My son has sprung out of bed at dawn to celebrate a new page on the calendar. His joy isn't about what he expects to *happen*. It's about the day.

This becomes a monthly ritual in our home. February 1, March 1, April 1: Ezra greets each arriving month with equal glee and fervor, his celebration echoing through the day. When he notices the month and day at the top of the newspapaper's front page; when he overhears the radio announcer say, "Good morning. It's Tuesday, July first"; when he spots the date on a bank's digital display board or writes it at the top of his homework sheet, he cannot help but whoop it up all over again: "It's February first!

"It's March first!"

"It's the first day of November!"

The turning of the seasons inspires the same kind of merriment: spring, summer, winter, fall. Ezra wakes up the family on the twenty-first of March or December with that same unrestrained joy:

"It's the first day of spring!

"It's winter now!"

Other children count down the days to Christmas or a birthday, to baseball spring training or to summer vacation. Ezra celebrates the simple passage of time.

His enthusiasm is easy to share, and we revel along with him. No matter what my mood when I awaken, it is difficult not to join him. As I wipe the sleep from my eyes, before I have the chance to bring to mind the worries of the day—mounting bills, pressures at work, a disagreement with Shawn—I do what Ezra does: I rejoice in the arrival of a new month.

In fact, long before he knew how to read a calendar, Ezra displayed an unusual attraction to the annual cycle, eagerly welcoming his favorite Jewish holidays—Passover, Purim, Hanukkah—and, before that, showing an extraordinary fascination with people's birthdays. Even at four or five, Ezra had one question he regularly asked almost everyone he met: "When is your birthday?"

He demonstrates a remarkable ability to memorize and recall the months (sometimes the days) in which birthdays fall. Driving him to preschool one day, I hear him reciting a combination of months and names. Then, listening more closely, I realize what he is doing: Ezra is enumerating the months of the year in order, and listing the birthdays he knows in each month.

Walking in the neighborhood, he encounters entire families we know and—without bothering with formalities like "hello"—rattles off the birth month of the mother, the father, the children—even the dog. Without any apparent effort, he commits to memory the birthdays of our immediate family, his four grandparents, his aunts and uncles and first cousins. Ezra isn't using flash cards or consulting a date book. He just knows.

One evening Shawn and I are in our bedroom talking when she mentions the name of one of our nieces. Abruptly, Ezra appears at the door, apparently having overheard.

"Shana is June," Ezra says, accurately. "Shana and Dalya are the only relatives that aren't in a thirty-one-day month."

As quickly as he appeared, he walks away.

The words tumble out so quickly that at first I'm not sure what he said, so I call after him and ask him to repeat it. He does.

"Shana is in June. Dalya is in November," he says. "Thirty days!

Everybody else has thirty-one days." And then he rattles off the names of the rest of our extended family, sorting them on the spot by month: "October is Uncle Mark and Abba and Papa; March is Aunt Marcia and Grandpa . . ." and on and on. Shawn and I look at each other. He's right. Everyone else in our family was born in a month with thirty-one days. Not only has he memorized the birthdays of at least seventeen relatives, he has taken the effort to perform a rudimentary statistical analysis, sorting the dates into categories another person might not have even considered or noticed.

It doesn't take a genius to figure out that nearly all of our relatives were born in months with thirty-one days. But it requires a certain kind of mind to notice. Hearing his observation about his cousins' birthdays gives me insight into the kind of thinking Ezra is doing in the long hours he spends on his own, avoiding social situations. It makes me pause to consider the mental processing that occupies him while the rest of us are talking. If he can mull over a list of ordinary dates and emerge with such a precise and magnificent insight, I wonder, what other astounding discoveries might be in his future?

I come to relish my periodic, precious glimpses into the extraordinary ways Ezra's mind makes sense of the world—particularly when he shows flashes of his powerful and unusual memory. When he is five years old and we are focused on early intervention—that is, finding him as much help as possible while his brain is still developing—he has a packed weekly schedule. It includes time at two different preschools (Temple Isaiah, with Dawn, and a therapeutic school called Smart Start) and various sessions with specialists. One morning I am shuttling him to his gymnastics class (taught by a man named Dave) when I think to remind him what's on his agenda.

"Ezzy," I say, "you know what you're doing today?"

He answers with a litany: "Dave's gym is one, Temple Isaiah is two, Smart Start is three, home is four, playing with water is five, dinner is six, dessert is seven, bath time is eight, reading books is nine, time to go to bed is ten, getting in Abba and Ima's bed is eleven." He has calibrated his routine down to the part where he regularly wakes up in the middle of the night and, unable to get back to sleep, sneaks under our covers.

"What's the number after eleven?" he asks.

"Twelve comes after eleven," I answer.

"Waking up is twelve, making pancakes is . . . what's after twelve?"

"Thirteen," I say.

"Making pancakes is thirteen. Sarah's gym is . . . What's after thirteen?"

"Fourteen."

"Sarah's gym is fourteen." Sarah's gym is what he calls the therapeutic center he visits for occupational therapy once a week. It's late in the school year, and he has been repeating his weekly and daily schedules for long enough that he keeps it all in his mind. Stunned, I ask him to start again.

"Dave is one, Temple Isaiah is two . . ."

I interrupt: "What's seven?"

He doesn't pause: "Dessert is seven."

"What's five?"

"Playing with water is five."

I almost pull the car over to the curb. At the time, Ezra seems to spend most of his waking hours in a fog. He is distracted, distant, and always in motion; he can't hold a conversation, echoes questions instead of answering them, looks off into space most of the time, flaps his hands, and resists attempts to engage him. He can't even count on his own past the number eleven.

And yet.

And yet he has been paying attention all along—so much so that he has internalized and mastered the patterns of his daily and weekly schedule; so much so that he knows it forward and—

"Ezzy," I ask, "can you tell me backward?"

Silence.

I help him out by starting: "Sarah's gym is fourteen, making pancakes is thirteen," I say.

He picks up from there: "Waking up is twelve, getting in Ima and Abba's bed is eleven . . ." He continues all the way to one.

Though I'm not sure how he does it, I come to realize that Ezra has an unusual, facile mind, an ability to absorb data, discern patterns, and keep track of it all. As with many of his traits, he reveals that aptitude inconsistently. He can't call on it at will—at least, not on request. But knowing that he has this well-concealed ability makes me regard him differently, and the closer I watch and listen, the more I see him display his nimble mind.

We are on a family visit to relatives in Portland when Shawn, at the wheel, stops the minivan at a traffic light. Ezra, then six, suddenly murmurs something.

"What, honey?" Shawn asks.

Ezra mutters four numbers: "One, two, four, two," he says.

"What's that?" I ask.

"That house has numbers."

I glance over at a brown one-story house where we are stopped. Above the door are the four digits of the address: 1242.

"That's the address," Shawn tells him.

"Bubbe has numbers on her gray house," he says casually. "Bubbe has two, seven, six, and four."

He is correct. The five of us have been staying for only a few days at my parents' house, the home of my childhood. Somehow, when we weren't looking, Ezra has memorized the street number: 2764.

"That's called the address," I repeat. "That's the number of the house. Do you know what our address is in Los Angeles?"

Ezra doesn't hesitate: "Nine, three, one, seven."

Correct.

"What's Nicholas's address?" Nicholas is the boy who lives in the gray two-story house next to ours.

"Nicholas is nine, three, two, three," he says. I'm stunned. "And Zach is nine, three, one, six." Zach lives across the street. Right again. Ezra isn't showing off. The tone in his voice isn't boastful. He is simply reporting facts, ticking off the digits as if recalling what he had for lunch. He doesn't even seem to notice how astonished Shawn and I—and even Ami—are at his ability to recall these numbers. We continue quizzing him. He knows the five-digit address of Dave's gym back home; of friends who once hosted us in Redlands; a relative's vacation house on the Oregon coast.

"How do you remember that stuff?" I ask.

He doesn't answer at first. I ask again.

"I just know," he says.

As Shawn keeps driving, I glance back at Ezra, now staring blankly at the passing traffic, the trees and buildings, and wonder what else he has been storing in his mind as he travels through the world.

Again and again, I am flabbergasted by Ezra's ability to recall information: names and places, experiences and numbers. As we drive in an unfamiliar neighborhood, he will suddenly speak up from the backseat: "Are we near Baskin-Robbins? . . . This is close to the Barnes and Noble." His uncanny internal GPS seems all the more astonishing because it so contrasts with his appearance, the way Ezra looks off into the air, the way he seems to be lost in his own thoughts and looping monologues. The more I experience his surprising memory, the more I come to realize that he is nearly always paying attention—perhaps even more so when he seems the most remote.

It isn't just places or dates he can commit to memory. When Ezra is nine, during a remodeling project we relocate to a compact apartment where the three boys share a cramped bedroom. The first night there, frustrated with the effort to settle them down to bed, I promise to tell them a special bedtime story.

With most of our books in storage—or not yet unpacked—I concoct one on the spot, a simple tale about three purple alligators and a magic waffle. To my surprise, the boys listen with unusual enjoyment and focus.

The next night they beg me to continue.

What began as a desperate measure soon evolves into a nightly ritual. Although I feel increasing pressure to create fresh plots and introduce new characters—an uncle visiting from Israel, a younger sister who can utter only one word—the boys are indiscriminate critics, lapping up each new chapter as I make it up.

I know the stories are accomplishing my goal of getting the boys into bed. What I don't realize is that Ezra is keeping close track. One evening many months after that first week in the apartment, he tells me he wants to make a list of all the alligators' adventures.

"I don't remember them all," I say.

"Let's make a list," he insists.

I sit down at the computer, and he dictates to me, recalling the plots one at a time, reminding me of the major developments—"When Jimmy became invisible . . . When Joey saw a penguin in the kitchen . . ." I conjured up the stories on the spot, but would feel hard-pressed to remember any details even hours later. Without hesitating, Ezra recalls one episode after another—"Episode four: when the alligators changed colors . . . Episode twenty: Mike the magician comes . . . Episode twenty-seven: when Cousin Fernando visited"—until he has recited the plots of twenty-nine chapters.

Does he have a photographic memory? Not exactly. Ezra has a *quirky* memory. Like almost everything else about Ezra's mind, it is unique, inconsistent, and subject to his whims, passions, and interests. One can't simply give Ezra lists or books or items to remember. His mind doesn't work that way. (In fact, he seems resistant to the kind of remembering that might be helpful in school.) Ezra's feats of memorizing seem effortless. If I find them astounding, it is partly because he doesn't work at remembering my alligator stories or the numbers he sees on buildings. He does it all so casually that he hardly understands the unusual mental prowess he possesses.

His memory reflects what matters to him. That becomes clear when he starts reading billboards. If we lived in Detroit, the massive signs lining our roads and freeways might have advertised for SUVs and pickups, and perhaps Ezra would have become an expert on the latest behemoths rolling off the assembly lines at Ford and Chevy. If our home had been in Las Vegas, maybe he would have mastered casinos.

But in Los Angeles, where practically every major thoroughfare is littered with billboards—massive, intrusive, abominable, inescapable—they nearly all advertise one thing: movies.

At some point early in his life, before we know he can read in a meaningful way, Ezra begins noticing the images from the animated movies he so loves—Shrek, Nemo, Piglet—on the massive advertisements he spies from his vantage point in the backseat. When he is in third grade, he begins talking about the sequel to the movie *Shrek*.

"*Shrek 2* is coming in May," he keeps repeating. An observation quickly evolves into a mantra. Day and night, he reminds us that *Shrek 2* will arrive in theaters in May. In Ezra's perception, the billboards aren't hints or even strong suggestions. They are marching orders. He never considers the possibility that he might *not* see the movie within days of its release any more than most people would consider bypassing Christmas. And he permanently etches the date—May 19, 2004—in his memory.

I don't know it at the time, but that date becomes one of the cornerstones of an abstract calendar Ezra is beginning to construct in his mind, an elaborate spreadsheet on which he quietly hangs tidbits of data, one at a time. Every time he views a new trailer at the theater or on TV, he silently takes note. Every time he spots a movie placard on the side of a city bus, every time he glimpses a film ad in the newspaper, Ezra tucks the information somewhere in the date book he is building in his brain: *Home on the Range*, April 2, 2004 . . . *Shark Tale*, October 1, 2004 . . . *The Incredibles*, November 5, 2004.

Just as when he memorized the street addresses or the alligator stories, Ezra does not appear to be exerting effort in building his mental almanac. Absorbing the information comes as naturally to him as breathing or eating his morning cereal. He can't stop himself; something compels him to attach numbers to movies.

That impulse manifests itself in surprising ways. On a visit to the Blockbuster store, Shawn and I are perusing the shelves, trying to agree on a movie to rent one Saturday evening, when I notice Ezra methodically making his way through the "family" section, grabbing one video box at a time and holding it close to his face like a butterfly collector examining a specimen. Keeping my distance, I watch for a few minutes as again and again, he repeats the same methodical motion: snapping up a video, scrutinizing its packaging, then replacing it on the shelf and moving on to the next. *Lion King. Mulan. Tarzan.*

"What are you doing?" I finally ask.

He doesn't respond, just repeats the odd, machinelike movements. I lean over and put my face close to his to get his attention.

"Ez, what are you doing?"

"Nothing I'm just . . ." He trails off.

"What are you looking at, Ezzy?"

"Running times," he says.

"Running times?" I ask.

"I'm seeing what the running times are," he says. "Now just let me be."

He keeps going, and I step away as my son continues plowing through the Blockbuster aisle.

It all goes into his catalog, the database in Ezra's head: premiere dates, running times, DVD release dates, names of studios and directors and voice-over actors. Sometimes he shares the information, usually at random moments, when nobody else is talking about movies.

"*The Many Adventures of Winnie the Pooh*. Running time: seventy-four minutes," he says while we wait for our order at the pizza place.

"*Toy Story 2* is ninety-two minutes," he says as he gets in the car after gym class.

At eight years old, Ezra cannot tell time, and if you were to ask him the length of his lunch break or how many minutes the ride home from school takes, he would answer with a blank stare. His fixation with movie running times isn't about time or schedule or even what might be the best length for a movie. It's another number for his chart.

Even in the realm of movie release times, he fixates on obscure bits of trivia with meaning only to him.

"I noticed something different, Abba," he announces to me one day in the car with great excitement. I expect that it might be about school or the house, but it's this: "Dreamworks running times have hours and minutes."

I can tell from his tone that this is important to him, but I'm not sure what he means.

"Like, *Finding Nemo* says one hundred minutes," he says. "But *Shrek* says it's one hour, twenty-nine minutes."

Okay. I think I understand. "Is it just *Shrek*?" I ask.

"No, all the Dreamworks movies say hours and minutes, but all the other studios just say minutes," he says. "I just *noticed* that!"

It's hard to know how to respond. I feel awe and wonder that my son's mind is so focused and discerning that he has spotted such a minuscule distinction. I am reminded of the singular journey of raising this boy. I know well the feeling of cheering on Ami when he catches a fly ball in a Little League game, the joy of admiring Noam's elaborate Lego creations. But this is something few parents experience: Ezra's ability to revel in what appear to be meaningless digits.

Of course, to him, they aren't meaningless at all.

To Ezra, the numbers—the addresses, the years and months, the hours and minutes—hold profound meaning. He invests in them the sort of significance other children place in the fine print on the back of baseball cards, or, say, their PlayStation scores. The difference is that children value those numbers because they are part of a shared experience, passions that connect them with other human beings; they trade cards with their friends; they play video games against opponents. The numbers are important because they provide entry points to conversations, to rivalries, to friendships.

Ezra, on the other hand, is building his mountain of obscure movie statistics on his own, invisibly assembling an internal almanac that only he can see, filled with data that has meaning only to him. He doesn't memorize the running time of *Shrek* to impress the other kids on the playground; that wouldn't occur to him. He doesn't do it to make conversation; he doesn't value that.

So why does he do it? Ezra craves the concrete. He has a deep need for structure, for things that won't change. His mind has trouble comprehending spoken language; lights feel too bright; tastes seem too strong; he feels uncomfortable in his own body; conversations and social situations leave him bewildered. The world is in constant flux, but the *Toy Story* DVD will always be eighty minutes long and the numbers above his grandmother's door will never change.

Mastering new realms of data brings him a feeling of calm that helps Ezra to feel at ease in the world. Yet the process is so invisible that I often don't know what new information he is committing to memory until he has already mastered it.

That's what happens with the "Disney Days" calendar. The calendar is a gift from my parents, who have a tradition of treating their grandchildren to tenth-birthday trips. They took our niece to a weekend in San Francisco, and accompanied Ami and a cousin—both passionate baseball fans at the time—to the All-Star game.

Not long before Ezra's turn, my parents visit us. Eager to inform Ezra about his upcoming trip, they sit down with him one afternoon at our computer.

"I want to show you something really special," my mother tells her grandson. It is difficult to grab his attention, until she gets him to focus on the Web site on the screen: Disney's Animal Kingdom, the theme park in Orlando.

"How would you like to go there?" my mother asks him.

"*Ooooh*, I would like that!" Ezra says.

"Well," she tells him, "Grandpa and I are going to take you there for your tenth birthday in January."

"Ooooh!" he says. "Can we go soon?" He is thrilled, but the trip is nearly three months away. My mother has planned for this with a small gift: a desktop calendar with a page for every day, each bearing a picture from a Disney movie. She has marked the page when they will fly to Orlando, to help him count down the days in anticipation.

Ezra keeps it on a shelf in a corner of his room, each morning remembering to tear off a new page, revealing the new day.

He maintains that practice for the weeks leading up to his trip, and then continues after his return. I don't pay much attention to the calendar until December of that year—more than a year after he first receives the calendar, and many months after the trip (a heavenly week for him). In his room one night, I notice the expired pages he has kept in a neat, orderly stack next to the calendar. I pick up a few to take a look.

"Put that back!" he demands.

I do. "What's wrong?" I ask.

"Leave it there. Don't touch those."

I'm not sure why.

"I like them there."

"Can I look at them?" I ask.

I can tell he doesn't want me to. Ezra's bedroom has an order that only he understands. I have always sensed that it makes him feel good—secure and comforted—to know where his most important possessions are.

"I just want to look for a second," I tell him. I pick up the stack and begin flipping through the pages, spotting a movie I like.

"*Finding Nemo*," I say.

"*Finding Nemo,* released May thirtieth, 2003," he replies.

I didn't even know I was quizzing him. He is across the room, nowhere near the calendar.

"How do you know that?" I ask.

"I just know," he says.

I thumb to another picture.

"*The Lion King*," I say.

He doesn't hesitate. "*Lion King*. June twenty-fourth, 1994."

I try a movie I'm not sure he has seen.

"*Lady and the Tramp*."

"*Lady and the Tramp*," he says, "release date June twenty-second, 1955."

I look at the stack—hundreds of pages—and wonder how many he could know. I grab another page at random and, instead of the movie title, read the date.

"What's on December fifteenth?" I ask.

"December fifteenth?" He thinks for a second, not more. "December fifteenth is *The Emperor's New Groove,* released December fifteenth, 2000."

I am about to flip to the next page when he speaks up again.

"There's a picture of Kuzco, the main character."

"How about November twenty-fifth?"

"November twenty-fifth? That's *Aladdin,* release date November twenty-fifth, 1992. There's a picture of Aladdin and the genie."

I call Shawn in from the other room. The two of us sit on Ezra's bed while he paces the room. We take turns thumbing through the pile of pages, amazed that he knows each one. I am even more astounded that he has accumulated all of this information without ever mentioning it.

The moment leaves me amused—and mystified. When has Ezra ingested all of this information? Late at night, after we put him to bed, has he hidden under his bedcovers, scrutinizing the hundreds of pages of the Disney calendar, drilling for hours, determined to master it all, reciting and reviewing until he has transferred it all into his brain? Or is it a more effortless process? Is my son able to snap a mental photograph of a page and store it in his brain, then access it on demand with his own internal version of Google?

I occasionally ask Ezra to explain how his memory works. The most he has been able to tell me, once, is this: "I can see it." When I try to probe deeper, he yields nothing.

"I just know. Now leave me alone."

Is it only the Disney calendar, I wonder, or is Ezra committing to memory all kinds of data without my even realizing it? As the years pass, will he surprise us by spontaneously reciting the menu from California Pizza Kitchen? The owner's manual for the computer? The contents of his history textbook?

And then there is this question: If he can remember the detailed contents of more than three hundred calendar pages, then why can't Ezra recall the names of the seven children in his fourth-grade class? When asked, he says one or two names as if he's guessing—"Rachel? Charlie?"— and then begs to be released from that arduous mental task. "It's hard to *remember*! Just let me *beeee*!" And why can he easily master lists of polysyllabic spelling words, but then not be able to recount a paragraph he perused just seconds earlier?

I contemplate the impossibly thin line between ability and disability. The very condition that makes it so difficult for Ezra to forge friendships, the same wiring that forces him into endless verbal loops and makes him uncomfortable in his own skin—that very condition makes possible these remarkable feats of memory. He finds it painfully difficult to do ordinary things like make eye contact in conversation, yet he can effortlessly do things that seem impossible to almost everyone else. Does that make Ezra's mind better or worse than anybody else's? That isn't the question in my mind. Instead, I wonder this: Does his memory need to make him more solitary and isolated? Or can it ever be the key to connecting Ezra to other people?

It is Ezra who answers that question, in his own unpredictable way. At a large family party when he is ten, he begins circulating through the hall and greeting other guests. His usual habit at such big events, which can overwhelm him with noise and activity, is to flee. Either he takes refuge in a quiet corner of the lobby with a picture book or he anxiously paces through the crowd, with no particular destination, arms tightly folded across his chest, occasionally jostling other guests or inadvertently bumping into a passing tray of hors d'oeouvres. This time, though, he surprises us by taking an interest in the other guests, asking a cousin or great-aunt, "What's your name, again?"

His second question is always the same: "What's your birthday?" Not exactly Emily Post's etiquette advice for social occasions, but it is such a welcome departure from his usual isolated behavior that I feel gratified by his efforts.

When he gets an answer, instead of just filing it in his mind, he responds with a movie title.

"June nineteenth?" he says. "A movie that came out on your birthday was *Mulan*, June nineteenth, 1998."

He says it so fast that most people don't hear or appreciate that in a split second, the boy has connected their birth date with a Disney movie.

"Say it again, Ezra, *slowly*," says Shawn, standing at his side.

". . . movie that came out your birthday's *Mulan*," he says, still rushing and skipping words.

Once they figure out what he is doing, the men and women who meet him are charmed and impressed—and often speechless.

"Oh, I haven't seen that," they say. "Is it good?" Usually, he is already gone, en route to jostle the next waiter. That is as much social contact as he wants.

I watch him do that again and again—always with the same enthusiasm, rushed pace, and lack of awareness of how abrupt it seems.

"Novemberthirteenth?" he says, slurring all of his words together. "Moviecameoutonyourbirthdaywas *Beauty and the Beast*, November thirteenth, 1991." Sometimes he throws in another fact: the DVD release date, say, or an actor's birthday. He has mastered not just Disney movies and not just animated pictures, but also the six movies of the *Star Wars* saga and, soon after, dozens of *Simpsons* episodes whose broadcast dates he has gleaned from his stack of *Simpsons* books or somewhere on the Internet.

At summer sleepaway camp—where Ezra participates in a remarkable program that integrates special-needs children with the general camp population—he gains a reputation for this skill, and children crowd around, calling out their birthdays. "Elianna!" he would say. "June twenty-third! Wide release of *Pocahontas!*" Or "Michael! *Robots*, released March eleventh, 2005!"

What at first seems like mere movie trivia comes to be something much more significant and powerful: a way to reach out to other people, a means for Ezra to use the remarkable workings of his mind to connect— in his idiosyncratic way. Months or years after making the link between person and movie, he remembers both, and reminds the person on each meeting.

The encounters are considerably less compelling when he discovers that an acquaintance was born in, say, mid-September or early January— annual lulls in animated movie releases. After excitedly asking, "When's your birthday?" Ezra reacts to the disappointing answer with a blank stare, a downward glance, and a few mumbled words that trail off—"Oh, I don't know any . . ."—as he quietly skulks away.

That often leaves the other person puzzling over what they've said wrong. I offer a shrug and a smile, and watch my son sauntering on, looking for the next person, the next birth date, the next new memory.

CHAPTER TEN

Chasing Elmo

Ezra is five. We bring the three boys to La Cienega Park, a green expanse of baseball fields and picnic tables tucked into a traffic-choked pocket of our neighborhood. Emerging from the minivan, the children quickly fan out into the bustling play area: Noam occupies himself in the sand pit, choosing a blue toy trowel we've brought to scoop fine granules into a red plastic bucket; Ami joins a ragtag group of boys scrambling up the sides of the jungle gym; Ezra is approaching the tire swing when, for a moment, I lose sight of him.

I have grown accustomed to the way he slips from our grasp, disappearing without warning in crowded places like supermarkets and the zoo. Still, it incites momentary panic. The busy boulevard abutting the park hums with traffic, and Ezra has little wariness of danger. I survey the crowd, looking from one child to another—the infant playfully cooing at her mother atop a picnic blanket; the two girls in pigtails clutching the bars of the spinning merry-go-round; the pudgy, red-faced boy descending the slide again and again.

Where is Ezra?

I finally spot him halfway across the playground. He's running, racing with some intention. And then I realize something: Ezra isn't alone. He is chasing after another child, a little boy about his age.

I'm stunned. In the dozens of times I have taken Ezra to the park, I have watched him do many things. He has fearlessly begged me to push him harder and higher on the swings; he has balanced his tiny body at precarious heights; he has bolted without warning, suddenly planting his palms over his ears and fleeing to take refuge behind the bronze sculpture at the distant reaches of another park. But I have never seen him do this: spontaneously play with a stranger.

"Shawn!" I call. She is sitting nearby, next to where Noam is digging in the sand. "Look at him!" I point toward Ezra, who is still dashing in pursuit of the boy in the white T-shirt and baggy navy shorts. As the child weaves around the play equipment—past the slide, the seesaw, the swing set—Ezra keeps tagging close behind. Shawn comes over and stands near me, and the two of us are speechless as we watch the scene unfold. I feel delight and excitement—as well as a sense of mystery: What has suddenly provoked Ezra to play with another little boy?

As the two kids swerve around the play structures and veer closer to us, I notice something: Ezra isn't exactly playing with the boy; his eyes are fixed on something on the boy's head. Looking around, I begin to figure out what is happening. The little boy has wandered from a birthday party under way at a nearby picnic table. Ezra's entire focus is on a conical paper party hat the boy is wearing. It's decorated with the face of Elmo, the friendly red monster from *Sesame Street*.

Ezra isn't chasing the boy. He's chasing Elmo.

What looked at first like a friendly game of tag is something much different. Watching closely, I'm not certain whether Ezra even *sees* the boy under the hat—or, for that matter, the other children bustling around him. Or his brothers. Or Shawn. Or me. He has focused his energies on the disembodied face of the red cartoon character he sees hovering over the playground.

I call out Ezra's name, trying to get his attention, and fearing he might topple the little boy in his attempt to snatch the hat. Ezra looks in my direction.

"Elmo!" he calls out. "I see Elmo!"

I'm rushing over to try to intervene when the boy outpaces Ezra, making his way back toward the birthday party. When I get to my son's side, he's standing in the playground sand, a delighted grin on his face, still looking in the little boy's direction.

"Look, Abba!" he says, pointing. "Elmo!"

Years later, I'm sitting next to Ezra at a matinee of a film called *Madagascar: Escape 2 Africa.* The movie is decent, but barely holding my attention. About forty-five minutes in, I shift my focus. Instead of watching the goofy animated animals on the screen, I zero in on my twelve-year-old son gazing at the action, mesmerized, in bliss. In the darkened theater, I watch Ezra's face, illuminated by the glow of the screen. Lost in the movie, he wears a facial expression of pure joy: his lips turn up in a grin; his eyes dance with delight while he watches the colors and shapes and listens to the sound track.

My grandmother used to do something like this. Though my Grandpa

Dave was an avid watcher of sports, Grandma Minnie could barely tell a baseball bat from a hockey stick. But she loved her husband. In the den of their apartment, she positioned her chair in the corner, just to the side of the TV: When Dave sat in his La-Z-Boy to watch the Red Sox, she would watch Dave.

That's what I have come to relish on these outings: to sit in darkened theaters watching animated animals and aliens and dinosaurs and robots. Sitting in crowded cinemas on opening weekend or in nearly empty theaters watching mediocre films, I watch my son, my child who almost everywhere else is twitching and anxious and uncomfortable, but who for these ninety minutes or so exudes true happiness.

Other children outgrow their interest in animated films, moving on to teen movies and the world of sophisticated entertainment: from *Finding Nemo* to *High School Musical* to *Lord of the Rings*. Ami and Noam were once as focused on animated fare as their brother, but Ami grows to love *Anchorman* and *Superbad*, and Noam becomes enamored with the Harry Potter films after he reads the books. Ezra has never moved on. Instead, as he has gotten older, he has become more and more preoccupied with the world of animated characters and movies—as if the entire universe of live-action movies doesn't exist, with one exception: the *Star Wars* saga. To him, Paul Newman is the voice of Doc, the town judge, in *Cars*, and Dustin Hoffman is the wizened martial arts master in *Kung Fu Panda*. What began as a source of childhood amusement has transformed over time into a fixation that touches almost everything he does. Just as, at five, he ran after the Elmo face without noticing the boy wearing the hat, he often seems to focus the majority of his conscious energies on Homer Simpson and Buzz Lightyear rather than the human beings around him.

He starts conversations with abrupt declarations about animated movies: "The character Red in the *Cars* movie doesn't talk very much," he'll say, or "Every character is in *The Simpsons Movie*, but Sideshow Bob does not appear." It's as if the conversation has been going on in his head for some time, but he's just thought to share his end of it aloud.

This happens all the time: It's six in the morning. I'm the only member of the family awake, and I'm alone in the kitchen, enjoying my morning tea, when I hear footsteps descending the staircase. It's Ezra. He approaches in his pajamas, still rubbing the sleep from his eyes.

"Morning, Ez," I say.

To which he answers: "Fiona is the princess of Far Far Away but then she falls in love with Shrek."

"How are you doing this morning?" I ask.

"Eddie Murphy is the voice of Donkey, who falls in love with Dragon, who doesn't have a name, just Dragon," he says.

It's as if he dwells mentally in an alternate reality populated by animated characters and an encyclopedia's worth of details about them. It's not daydreaming, in the sense that daydreams divert your attention from the real. I imagine that it's more like Ezra is watching a movie in his mind. On his mental screen, he sees not an actual movie, but the entire animated universe he has accumulated. Only, to him, it's vivid and real.

When you watch a movie in a theater, you're absorbed with the reality of the movie on the screen, but every once in a while, you shift your consciousness and become momentarily aware that you are sitting in a chair in a theater. You notice the glowing green exit sign, the silhouetted heads of the men and women in the rows in front of you, the occasional patron shuffling off to buy popcorn. This is how Ezra goes through his days. As his body is in school or at home or in the car, he is watching, say, *The Incredibles* on his internal screen. Occasionally, he takes note of the world around him: the teachers trying to attract his attention, the brothers operating in his orbit just beyond his focus, or his mother or me. Speaking to him can be like whispering into the ear of that person mesmerized by a movie. He can hear, but he's focused on the movie's sound track—and he can find the interruption annoying and even highly aggravating.

As soon as Ezra ascertains the date of an upcoming animated feature, that date becomes a focal point, more prominent in his mind than a birthday or school vacation. At some point our family adopts the practice of attending his movies on the first Sunday afternoon following their release. He comes to rely on and expect that, asking repeatedly for reassurance that his plan will come to pass.

"Will we see *Chicken Little* on November sixth, Abba?"

"I hope so, Ez."

"*Will* we?" he asks, more agitated. "Say we *will* see *Chicken Little* on November sixth, Abba!"

"Of course we will."

"Yeah. Right. Of course we will. Of *course* we will see *Chicken Little* on November sixth, Abba."

He craves that reassurance, just as he thrives on his visits to the zoo and seeing that all of the animals are where they are supposed to be. He finds it comforting and reassuring that his movies are where they are supposed to be. It's control over chaos. It gives him a powerful sense of security and comfort to know that *Shark Tale* will hit theaters on October 1, 2004, and that on the afternoon of October 3, he will be in a dark theater in the Pacific Culver Stadium theater watching, with a tub of popcorn on his lap.

Of course, that can make life challenging when things don't go as he expects. Ezra sometimes makes his mental plans around more obscure animated movies without making sure that the adults in his life have fully registered the schedule.

"Abba, will we see *Horton Hears a Who* on March sixteenth?"

"I'm not sure, Ez. We may have something else that day."

"You're not *sure*!?" he says, his voice rising an octave and gaining volume quickly. "But you *must* become sure!"

"I just don't know yet, Ez."

"Yes, we *will* see it on March sixteenth," he says dramatically but with utter sincerity. "How could you *do* this?"

"Ezzy, I'm sure we'll see it," I say. "I just don't know when yet."

"Don't block the day," he says. *Block the day*. That's his original phrase for when someone tries to alter a plan that was set firmly in his mind. "Say that we will see *Horton Hears a Who* on March sixteenth."

The conversation goes on like this until I can defuse the situation—usually after some fuss, and even some tears. He cries about these things because it's all real to him—as real as it was in that moment at his third birthday party, when I discovered him alone in his bedroom acting like Tigger from *Winnie the Pooh*.

It's also the structure he finds appealing. Around age five, he somehow teaches himself which characters belong to which studios.

"Daffy Duck, he's not *Disney*!" Ezra says, appalled that anyone could make such an obvious error. "He's *Warner Brothers*!" I never figure out how a five-year-old boy with limited ability to communicate came to understand that Disney and Warner and Hanna-Barbera and Fox each has its own stable of characters, but he does, and he masters them all the way other boys master baseball lineups.

Why is he so focused on sorting out these cartoon faces? Perhaps because his brain has such difficulty processing and interpreting the faces of the human beings around him. What comes intuitively to others—understanding the emotion reflected in a particular smile or smirk or furrowed brow—is baffling to him. When he is five and six, we spend countless bath times (when he'll sit still in the comfort of the warm water) playing games of Name That Face to teach Ezra expressions like "happy," "sad," "curious," and "excited." When he grows older, I often catch him pausing from brushing his teeth to practice facial expressions on his own, gazing into the bathroom mirror as he manipulates his cheeks and eyebrows with his fingertips to demonstrate.

Cartoon characters don't deal in subtle nuance, and Ezra has no trouble reading Elmer Fudd's scowl, or the frightened eyes of Nemo, or the angry, creased forehead of Homer Simpson. So it's no surprise that he would rather spend time looking at the faces he understands. (On occasions when I'm frustrated with him, he often reacts by trying to convince me to change my facial expression before anything else: "Abba, your eyebrows are down! Put them back up!"—as if altering my features will instantly change my mood, or his consequences.)

Besides the visual appeal, there's an auditory factor to Ezra's attraction to animation. He often flees from ordinary social exchanges because he has such difficulty deciphering the spoken language he hears. The words become garbled as his brain struggles to interpret them, causing such anxiety that he retreats and avoids conversation. At the movies, he can take in dialogue without anyone expecting him to respond—and he can play a DVD over and over until he understands the words and keep listening until he commits dialogue to memory. That explains why for several years of his childhood it's almost impossible to engage Ezra in dialogue, but he will routinely spout movie lines like the one from *The Emperor's New Groove*, "Llama? He's supposed to be dead!" or another from *Toy Story*—"Mrs. Potato Head! Mrs. Potato Head!"—that usually put him into hysterics, for reasons I cannot fathom.

One morning when he's four, Ezra crawls into our bed and starts to tell a story. It's an elaborate tale about Simba, the patriarch from *The Lion King*. I start asking him questions and for once he reacts not by shutting down and fleeing, but by answering.

"Where does Simba live, Ezra?" I ask.

"He lives in the pride lands. Yeah, he's going to run in the pride lands."

"And then what?"

"And he's going to see his friend Nala."

"Good! And then what?"

"They're going to play, yeah, and then they'll find Zazu."

The exchange continues, leaving Shawn and me surprised at his newfound ability to tell a story spontaneously, until he concludes:

"That's the end of our story. If you'd like to hear it again, just turn the tape over."

As he grows and develops, his mental catalog of movie dialogue snippets provides the basis for an additional form of communication within our family. After Ezra repeats a line of Disney dialogue a few dozen times, the other boys are first amused, then annoyed, and then they join in, reciting the dialogue back to him: "Three days? What about lunches?" they say, mimicking Winnie the Pooh trapped in Rabbit's hole. Or the would-be superhero's bit from *The Incredibles*: "Where is my supersuit?" The lines take on lives of their own, like a joke told so many times it gets old, and then absurdly funny. What started as Ezra's involuntary tics morph into a nonsensical secret language that our children share with one another.

Of course, while movie snippets are better than silence, they are hardly real conversations. When we ask his doctor for advice about steering Ezra away from the habit, she suggests simply to label the practice *movie talk* and discourage it.

"Oh, that's *movie talk*," I say the tenth time he repeats the same line from *Cars* instead of answering my question. "I don't want to hear movie talk. I want to hear *Ezra* talk."

Sometimes that works. Sometimes it frustrates him. Sometimes he catches himself in midsentence: "Oh, that's movie talk. You don't want to hear that?" he says, half asking.

I often think that, given the choice, my son would opt to live in a land of animation, free from the fetters and demands of living, breathing human beings. In some ways, he already does. More than once I have happened into Ezra's bedroom late at night to put clean laundry in the closet or straighten up, and caught him talking in his sleep—to characters from whatever movie is preoccupying him that week. Around age twelve, when he starts remembering and describing his dreams, he tells me one morning he dreamed the night before about finding himself alone at the home of some family friends late at night, somehow charged with the chore of cleaning up the place before they returned home.

"Then there was a knock on the door," he says.

"Who was it?" I ask.

"It was Homer and Marge Simpson."

I imagine that would delight Ezra. No, he says, the Simpsons created a huge mess and left Ezra to clean it up.

"Do you have lots of dreams with animated characters?" I ask.

"I think so," he says. "Most nights."

I make efforts to join Ezra in celebrating his beloved animated world, to build a relationship based on what he values. It's not always easy. Often, my attempts—even those that seemed most benign and simple—fail.

When Ezra is six, I take him to Disneyland. It's a hot August day; Ami will be visiting another theme park with his day camp, and Noam is still too young for the more dizzying theme park rides, so just the two of us head for Anaheim, about forty-five minutes from home. It's his first visit, and my first in many years. Since Ezra is so captivated by Disney movies (at the moment, he's lingering in his *Winnie the Pooh* phase), I am certain that he will revel in encountering a supersize Mickey Mouse wandering the streets of the Magic Kingdom. As we barrel down Interstate 5 through dull, industrial stretches of Orange County in the blue Camry, I envision him posing with Goofy and Pluto and goggling at his beloved Pooh friends in full, gigantic costume. I wonder how I will ever pry him away once he comes across these larger-than-life, colorful creatures.

I don't need to worry about that. He devours the thrill rides, particularly the Mad Tea Party, where he chooses a red cup and together we grasp the circular handle, spinning ourselves until I am on the verge of vomiting and Ezra looks calmer and happier than I have seen him in months. (Spinning always has a soothing effect on him, magically lulling his body.) When the ride finally slows down and the cup stops spinning, I feel relieved and Ezra begs for more.

"Again! Again!"

It's when we head to Disneyland's Toontown section, where the costumed Disney characters walk about, that I am taken by surprise. From a distance, I spot a line of children waiting to visit with Mickey Mouse. An expression of worry flashes across Ezra's face.

"Come on, Ezra," I say. "He wants to meet you!"

We're still a hundred feet from the five-foot rodent when Ezra catches sight of the protruding black ears and the gigantic, eager eyes. Just at the moment when I expect him to break into a run—forward—he stops walking, plants his sneakers, and begins backing up.

"I don't want to . . ." he says.

"Of course you do!" I say. "That's why we *came*."

"No!" he insists, then fully turns his body, walking quickly in the opposite direction.

In another part of the park, I spot his favorites, Tigger and Winnie the Pooh—vivid bursts of bright orange and golden yellow fabric—signing autographs for a crowd of tykes.

"Wanna go see Pooh?" I ask.

Ezra looks as nauseous as I felt on the teacups ride. The same boy who just minutes earlier smiled and laughed through Splash Mountain, with its terrifying waterfall plunge, suddenly looks panicked and meek, eyeing the gigantic cartoon characters as if they are armed thugs.

Witnessing how utterly unsettling the encounter is becoming, I grab Ezra's hand and together we scurry away through the crowd, moving on to the next ride. At Disneyland, though, it is difficult to avoid large costumed creatures. We're walking together on a quiet pathway near the Sleeping Beauty Castle when suddenly another one appears from behind a building. It's the Beast from *Beauty and the Beast*—seven feet of artificial fur, protruding horns, and terrifying fangs. Ezra reacts by simply slapping his palms over his eyes, crying "No! *No!*"

He's had enough.

On the drive home, I contemplate how I could have been so wrong— why the parts I expected to be his favorites turned out to be nearly torturous for him. Perhaps what draws him to his animated movies is the retreat they provide him from reality, which assaults his system with overwhelming sensations, making him feel anxious and out of control. What appeals to him is the predictability of that world, the lack of surprises. Ezra doesn't want Winnie the Pooh to exist in the same plane of reality that causes him such discomfort. He wants his characters in the videos where they do the same things and say the same words over and over and over. What appeals to him is a world where the characters don't ask anything of him, where things are predictable, and where Ezra feels in control.

One way he exerts control is by gaining a command of the material. When Ezra memorizes dialogue, pores for hours over animation books, commits premiere dates to memory, or puzzles through movie plots— when he pours his energy and efforts into these pursuits, I feel him striving to gain a sense of mastery and control.

For a time, when he is nine, his obsession becomes Wallace & Gromit, the clay characters created by a British animator named Nick Park. Practically overnight, he switches his enthusiasm from Disney and Pixar to this eccentric English inventor and his silent, mouthless white dog. He sees the movie *Wallace & Gromit: The Curse of the Were-Rabbit*, a quirky tale involving an entire world foreign to Ezra: magical garden gnomes, Rube Goldberg contraptions, a vicar, a vegetable-growing contest. Ezra begins compulsively drawing pictures of the characters, and I notice him squirreling away pieces of loose-leaf paper in a nightstand drawer.

One night when he's sleeping, I open it and find scores of sheets of paper, all densely decorated with hundreds of Wallace & Gromit drawings and sentence fragments describing the various characters: "Gromit doesn't make any noise at all. He doesn't talk and doesn't have a mouth."

I show them to Shawn, and the two of us sit together and flip through the stack, an enigmatic window into how he is struggling to understand this miniature universe. The scrawl on the pages reveals his obsessive thoughts but they also divulge something else: Lacking the kind of statistics he likes to gather from the nutrition panels of cereal boxes or listings he has devoured in animal almanacs, he is trying to create his own database. Ezra is endeavoring to make sense of things, to achieve a sense of control.

There is another way to control an animated world: by creating it yourself. With his consistent and pervasive fascination with animation, I sometimes wondered when Ezra was in elementary school whether he might ever be able—or willing—to try creating animated characters of his own. He struggles with fine motor control issues that hinder his handwriting, but occasionally he experiences bursts of interest in drawing, periods when he obsessively fills sketchpads and reams of paper with cartoonish drawings of animals, colorful alphabets, and rainbows. For a few months around age nine, he becomes enamored with billiard balls, memorizing their colors, the solids and stripes, and using felt markers to draw them over and over.

Soon after that, he discovers Charlie Brown and begins filling the same pads and sheets with remarkably detailed and accurate knockoffs of Charles Schulz's Peanuts cast: Snoopy and Woodstock, Lucy and Linus. He is copying from Schulz's drawings in a couple of anthologies he received as birthday gifts, but his renderings are not childlike stick figures but extraordinarily faithful and detailed imitations. He fills one pad after another, day and night.

And then he stops. He won't draw, and even when we encourage him to, and when he tries, his drawings become cruder, his efforts less focused.

"Why won't you draw?" I ask.

"It doesn't look the same," he says. He has trained himself to so scrutinize the details of his beloved animated characters that he won't tolerate inexact replicas—even his own. He goes back to looking, only occasionally showing an interest in drawing.

In the summer when he's twelve, our family is visiting Portland when my mother arranges a meeting for Ezra. Months earlier, she met a visual artist who runs a nonprofit called CHAP—Children's Healing Art Project—that encourages kids coping with serious illnesses and other challenges to create art. When she learned that the program teaches animation, she mentioned her grandson, and the director suggested that Ezra visit sometime.

"Don't get your hopes up," I tell her that morning. "Ezra likes talking about animation, but I have no idea whether he'll be willing to do any." I have become frustrated myself with his recent refusal to draw—particularly since he once showed such promise. It's the kind of impasse Ezra frequently hits, and from which it can be impossible to budge him.

"Well," says Mom, "it's worth a try."

Ezra and I find our way to the studio, in a cavernous loft space on the top floor of an old brick warehouse that also houses a brewery. There, we meet Frank, the director, who sports a funky goatee and greets us with enthusiasm. While Ezra sweeps through the space as if he lives there, examining the colorful canvases on the walls and making his way into closets and bins, I tell Frank briefly about my son.

"He knows everything about animation, but he tends to get stuck in his own thoughts," I say. "So I don't know . . ."

Frank waves me off.

"He'll do great," he says, and dismisses me. "We'll see you in a couple hours."

I leave my cell phone number, and, with some hesitation, head down-stairs, certain that Frank will call within a few minutes to report that Ezra is unable to focus. I simply know that for all of Frank's purported skill, he won't get through to my son.

I drive to Powell's Books, just a few blocks away. Ten minutes pass. Twenty. Thirty. I check to make sure my phone is switched on. I contem-plate calling to check in. After an hour and forty-five minutes, nobody has called, and I return to the brick warehouse and ascend the stairs, certain that when I get to the studio, Ezra will be zoned out on a com-puter, waiting for me.

"He's doing great," the woman who works with Frank says when I arrive.

"Really?" I ask.

"Amazing," she says, pointing to the back of the studio. "Go look."

In the next room, I discover Ezra, deeply ensconced in work with a teacher who introduces himself as Steve.

"We're not quite done," Steve tells me.

"Has he . . ." I don't finish. Steve just smiles and nods with approval.

I watch Ezra mold tiny clay balls he has created, manipulating them in a small box next to a camcorder on a tripod. He is creating clay animation. His own Wallace & Gromit.

"I'm doing *great*, Abba!" Ezra says with enthusiasm.

Each ball is a different color, like the pool balls he once compulsively drew. He has made a house from construction paper and attached a yellow sliver of a moon against the backdrop. I watch for a few minutes as Ezra, with only minimal prompting from Steve, shoots the final few moments of his film. Ezra is completely absorbed in the process—not pacing, not spinning, not displaying anxiety—and clearly pleased with himself.

When they finish, Steve connects a cable from the camcorder to a laptop.

"It'll take a minute to download," he says. Now Ezra paces the creaky hardwood floors as we wait. When Steve is ready, I gather around with the two of them and Frank to watch.

Ezra has called his movie *The Twelve Balls*. One at a time, the tiny clay spheres, each a different color, roll into the house. The door closes behind the last. Then another ball shows up—this one brown, with pointy protruding ears.

"Wait, don't forget about me!" says Ezra's voice on the sound track. The door opens, and the little doggy ball hurries inside. The credits roll. I look at Ezra, a huge smile crossing his face. The whole film lasts all of twelve seconds, but it tells a sweet story and has many of Ezra's loves: animation, a variety of colors, even a dog.

As we descend the stairs, I take in the aroma of hops emanating from the brewery below and think about how, after years of obsessing about animation, Ezra has taken his first steps in a new direction.

"Abba," he says as we reach the car, "I'm an animator now. You're very proud of me."

Indeed I am.

CHAPTER ELEVEN

Is Your Dog Friendly?

I steer into the parking lot, find an open space, slide open the minivan door—and they're off. Ezra hops out, grasping the leash as Sasha, our mini shepherd mix, barrels past a baseball diamond and an asphalt basketball court toward the familiar grassy slope: our neighborhood dog park.

This is the highlight of the week for Sasha and Ezra alike, the moment they both come alive with excitement and pure joy. Sasha dashes toward a spot in the shade of a eucalyptus tree, where she playfully runs circles around a Chihuahua, until an energetic Labrador retriever lures her away. Ezra extends both arms upward, twirls in place a couple of times, and then begins surveying the crowd like a schoolteacher taking roll.

"Look, it's Otto!" he calls to me, pointing out an ivory-colored German shepherd. Ezra rushes toward the dog's owner, a twentyish fellow who, as usual, is tossing gnarled yellow tennis balls for his pet to fetch. After a quick hello, Ezra bounds across the grass to greet a woman nearby.

"Where's Bagel?" he asks. She points across the lawn to her Boston terrier, and Ezra skips with glee to greet the pooch with a pat on the head.

As it happens, ours isn't a bona fide, officially designated dog park. It is against the law in Los Angeles County to let a dog off leash in public—a misdemeanor punishable by a $113 fine. This is the only illegal thing I do routinely: come to this grassy expanse dotted with sycamore trees with my son and our dog. I do roll through an occasional stop sign and make illicit U-turns now and then, but I have been caught for that. One afternoon I am returning with Ezra from visiting a petting zoo outside L.A. when a patrol car stops me. As the trooper arrives at my window, Ezra speaks up from the backseat.

"Why is he talking to us?" he asks.

I start to answer, but he's not listening. Not pausing, Ezra blurts out something about the hog he was petting just minutes earlier. Not a great idea to mention the word *pig* to a state trooper with a badge and a gun. (Fortunately, the officer doesn't hear.)

I never would have imagined that either Ezra or I would become dog-park regulars. When the boys were young, they often played at the nearby playground. As I pushed them on swings or they climbed on the elaborate jungle gyms, I would occasionally look up and wonder who these people were across the park, gathered in clutches, holding coffee mugs in one fist and leashes in the other, surrounded by dogs and dog poop. It wasn't my crowd.

As for Ezra, his early encounters with dogs do not seem to foretell a deep connection with the species. His difficulty controlling his impulses keeps landing him in trouble. When he is eight, we drop in on friends one rainy weekend afternoon and Ezra becomes intrigued with their elderly golden retriever.

"Don't get too close; he's a little out of sorts," our friend Avi warns. It's too late. In another room, Ezra has already wrapped his body around the decrepit creature. Seconds later, his scream echoes through the house.

"Owww!" he cries, running toward us with both hands clutching his nose. "He bit me! He bit me!" he keeps repeating, as Shawn tries to offer comfort and Avi applies a bandage.

If Ezra learns from the experience, it is difficult to tell. Three years later, staying with relatives in Boston, he becomes enamored with my cousin Ted's pair of dachshunds, high-strung and temperamental dogs that are much less enthused about him. No matter how many times Ted patiently warns Ezra to keep a safe distance, my son cannot restrain himself. Each time Ezra slips from sight in the house, I discover Ezra crouching on the floor, attempting to play with Willi, the older dog, as Reese, the younger one, growls menacingly nearby.

One evening as we are dressing to head out for a family dinner, Ted arranges a complex of gates to confine the dogs to the kitchen. Before anyone can notice, Ezra has taken a long, not-so-careful stride over the barrier to play. As predicted, Reese greets him with a nip on the heel. Despite the warnings, despite his previous experience, Ezra is flabbergasted, bouncing away on one foot while he grasps the injured ankle.

"I just wanted to play!" he says, voice full of enthusiasm despite the snap. "Why does Reese have to be so rebellious?" Then, looking over the gate and directly at the skinny, diminutive canine, he asks: "Why do you have to be such a rebellious cousin dog?"

Again and again, Ezra demonstrates how impulsive behavior and pets can be an unfortunate mix—though usually it is the pets that pay the price. More than once when he is young, he is at a family friend's house when the sight of a goldfish piques his interest. The first time, when he is six, Shawn and I both hear the crash of shattering glass, run to the scene, and discover shards of what had been a fishbowl on one family's TV room floor, while Ezra cowers in the corner.

"I just wanted to see what it *felt* like," he says.

He learns to be more careful when he's eleven and gets his own pair of white mice acquired at PETCO for $1.99 apiece. He names them Mia and Tia, after characters in his favorite movie, Pixar's *Cars*. He keeps them for a couple months on a bookshelf in his room, helping to clean the cage, and taking responsibility for feeding them a single food pellet when he awakens each morning, until one Saturday morning when I'm eating breakfast and I hear his panicked cry from upstairs.

"Abba, I think Tia is dead!"

Before I can even stand up, Ezra comes bounding down the steps, a concerned look on his face, his right hand extended and cupping something small and white.

"Is it dead?" he asks.

It certainly appears to be. Once we settle Ezra down, I try to get him to explain.

"How did it happen?" I ask.

"She was old?" he says, more asking than telling. At eleven, he still has a juvenile understanding of death: It is something that happens to old people—and animals.

"She was old?" I repeat. "Is that why she died?"

He looks at me. "No?"

"How did the mouse die?"

"She just died."

I wait.

"She was in the window and she died."

"In the window? What do you mean?"

For reasons he cannot explain, he took the pair of mice from their cage and put them in the space between his bedroom window and the outer window screen. Then he lowered the window sash, not realizing, perhaps, that the tiny creature was in the way.

"It was an accident," Ezra says. "I didn't *mean* to." He seems genuinely sad, even bewildered. He asks again, "Was Tia old?"

"What do you think?" I ask.

"No," he says. And then, after a pause: "Can we get a new mouse?"

"Well, first I want you to understand what happened."

"Tia died."

"How do you feel about that?"

"I feel sad."

"Are you okay?"

"I'm okay," he says in a forlorn, resigned tone. "Tia died."

Ezra's impulsiveness around pets doesn't reach a nadir until shortly after that, when we acquire our cat, a gray-and-white shorthair the boys name Dash. At first the kitten provides a point of commonality among our three boys, who take turns luring him with pieces of string and compete for time snuggling with him on the couch. The cat inspires the best in them, and brings our family a new sense of peace and calm.

Until the thump at the bottom of the steps.

I am sitting alone, reading a magazine in the family room that evening, when, out of nowhere, I hear the sound, a dull thud on the oak floor at the foot of the stairway. A few seconds later: a muted meow. I look up to see Dash, still a kitten, limping from the spot, gingerly making his way across the hardwood.

I leap to my feet and run up the stairs, stopping on the landing to look upward, where I spot Ezra peering down from between the balusters. His expression is neither gleeful nor guilty. He's just looking.

"What happened?" I demand.

"I threw Dash," he says coolly.

"Why did you do *that*?" I ask.

Nothing. Now Shawn has emerged from another room and Ami and Noam come from the den, where they have been watching *SpongeBob* and heard the commotion.

"What's going *on*?" Ami yells. Noam looks incredulous. Shawn scoops up the hobbled kitten, the three of them closely examining the victim while I focus on the alleged perpetrator.

"Ezra, what were you thinking?"

"I'm *sorry*!" he says.

"Do you see what you did?" I say. "You hurt the cat."

"I didn't throw Dash down," he says. I wait a moment for an explanation. "I threw him *up*."

I look at the hard wooden stairway, in two flights with a landing between floors, and realize what he means: He tossed Dash upward toward the ceiling, so that the cat arced and then landed—on its feet, surely—midstaircase.

I shake my head. "Why?"

"I'm *sorry*," he says, and then he says what he wants me to say: "It's okay. Say, 'It's okay.'"

"It's *not* okay," I say. "You could have killed him."

I think of the lengthy contract the SPCA lady insisted we sign before she would give us the cat. No declawing; no outside time (felines in our area commonly fall victim to coyotes or cars); no abuse of any kind. I do not recall a specific clause about tossing down stairways, but I figure it was implied.

The after-hours veterinarian feels around Dash's extremities, examines his eyes and ears, and determines that the kitten will survive. He has escaped without significant injuries. Relieved, I drive home, pondering whether Ezra will ever be able to learn to control his rash behavior around pets. I know these incidents—the run-in with Reese, with the mouse, and this one with the cat—have happened in spite of his intentions. It is no different from the way he involuntarily flapped his arms as a preschooler, or how he sometimes can't stop himself from blurting out comments about people's weight or hair. Ezra doesn't mean to do these things to animals. He cannot yet stop himself.

That is clear from his encounters with dogs. Walking around the neighborhood, he lavishes attention on almost every mongrel he encounters, and develops an exhaustive knowledge of their breeds, traits, and vital statistics. He finds it impossible to saunter past a person walking a dog without accosting them both. Spotting an elderly woman approaching from up the block with her poodle, Ezra abruptly sits himself cross-legged in their path on the sidewalk. When they near, he grabs the high-strung animal as it approaches and tries to cuddle it in his lap while the owner looks on with alarm.

He develops a routine inquisition to which he subjects anyone he spots with a canine:

"Excuse me, can I pet your dog?

"What kind of dog is your dog?

"Male or female?

"How old?"

Hearing the age, Ezra always replies with a commentary. "*Ooh*, a puppy!" Or "She's *old!*" Or simply: "Middle-aged." (Of course, most people don't think of their dogs as middle-aged, a designation that brings to mind AARP membership, argyle sweaters, and hot flashes.)

Not being a master of social nuance, he often follows up, to my chagrin, with another question: "When is he going to *die?*"

It is that last part that gives dog owners pause. *When is he going to die?* "Ummm . . ."

"Ezra!" I say, feigning shock that my own son has uttered such an insensitive question.

"I think he'll be around for a while," the person might respond.

"He's not going to *die* soon?" Ezra says. Then he reassures himself: "No, he'll be around for a few years." Sometimes Ezra launches into a monologue about the data about canine longevity he has gleaned from his books: A small dog like a Chihuahua can live up to eighteen or nineteen years, while a Labrador might survive only eleven or twelve.

That makes it awkward when Ezra learns that a larger dog has reached the advanced age of twelve or thirteen.

"Oooh, she's going to pass away *soon!*" he'll say.

It's at that point that I usually smile at the person and pull Ezra away.

"Ezra, stop!" I say under my breath. "They don't want to think about when their dog is going to *die!*" To him, it isn't a sensitive matter, just an objective piece of information, like the country of origin or average weight.

I try to teach him to offer a compliment—something like, "Beautiful dog!"—instead of predicting a dog's imminent demise. But sometimes it comes out with such exuberance or such awkward intonation that people still find his comments unsettling.

Most seem to understand, though, especially when they see that Ezra enjoys dogs so much that he hunches on all fours, lets the pooches lick him all over his face, and often licks them back. (The same neurological wiring that makes him overly sensitive to sudden sounds and makes him crave hot foods causes him to seek out sensations from which other people recoil—like the feeling of being licked by a slobbery dog.)

And they are delighted and impressed when, on later encounters, he spouts from memory their pets' vital statistics: name, gender, birth date, temperament. He almost never forgets a dog. Ezra knows the names of only a handful of neighbors, but he knows Ollie the shih tzu, Milo the terrier mix, and he always bounds out our front door and barrels toward the sidewalk when he spots Rox, a spirited local Dalmatian, dragging his owner past. He rarely sees any of their owners at the market or a restaurant without asking after the dog the way other people might inquire about grandchildren or work. "How's your dog Fiona? She turned three!" Or "Is Griff still itching from fleas?"

A couple who move in up the block is charmed by the way Ezra lights up at the sight of their golden retriever, wrapping his entire body around the animal with full abandon as if he were embracing a beloved friend, and smothering the pooch with kisses.

"You really need to get him a dog," the woman says.

"We know," Shawn and I say in unison, though we have no plans to do so; we feel like our hands are full with the boys.

Taking pity, they tell Ezra he can borrow the dog anytime. He likes that idea, so on a few weekend afternoons, I tag along as he proudly holds the leash and lets the retriever lead him at a trot, weaving through the neighborhood, Ezra scrambling to keep up, an elated grin across his face.

*   *   *

In spite of our hesitation, seeing Ezra so savor his time with the dog convinces us that our family should indeed consider acquiring one, mostly as a companion for Ezra, a mate in lieu of the human friends he still doesn't seem to be making.

We begin looking at the nearest shelter, a county facility not far from home. It seems to go on forever, with cage after cage containing sad dogs with pleading eyes. Ezra wants every last one: the rangy Doberman, the snarling pit bull, the yappy poodle. He can find no fault, sitting on concrete floors and looking at the dogs eye-to-eye and—defying our instructions—sticking his fingers in the kennel for the dogs to lick. At some, he rests a cheek against the wire to let dogs lap at his face. On the way home, he recollects a dozen of the pooches by name and breed—the beagle named Lucky, the chow chow named Buzz—but cannot settle on just one.

At a rescue organization in Beverly Hills, the volunteer looks over our application form and our family, asks us a few questions, then says he has two dogs that might be perfect. The first, a Dalmatian, doesn't seem to respond to anything we say.

"Oh, he's deaf," the volunteer finally says. "I thought I had mentioned that."

The second dog is a Labrador missing an eye. The boys find that unsettling. Shawn—always looking for ways to make the world better—feels pity for the dog, and tells me that adopting it would be a lovely expression of our values.

I shake my head. "I have enough problems," I say with a smile, "without a special-needs dog."

Shawn takes ownership of the search, shuttling Ezra the next weekend to another series of rescue shelters. She phones Sunday afternoon from one.

"We found the dog," she says, a smile in her voice.

"How do you know?" I ask.

"This dog is licking Ezra all over the place," she says. "You have to come see her."

I drive over with Noam. Shawn meets us at the door and walks us in, past rows of cages of cats, through a compact warren of kennels holding dogs of various breeds and sizes, to a window looking into a small cage. There, Ezra sits on the floor, looking into the eyes of a midsize, year-old mongrel with the coloring of a German shepherd, dark, soulful eyes, the ears of a Labrador, a spotted tongue, and a tight, slender frame.

"This is the dog," Shawn says. The shelter lets the four of us walk the dog around the block. When we pause at a grassy sidewalk median, Ezra sits cross-legged and lets the dog lick him, and Ezra licks back.

I smile at Shawn. "This is the dog," I agree.

The boys name her Sasha. Over time, I watch Ezra, eager to see how finally realizing his dream of having his own dog will transform him—hoping he will develop a close tie with the dog, unlike anything he has experienced.

I do see a change, but not the one I expected. Ezra reacts to dog ownership the way he responds to almost everything else he deems important: He steps up his cataloging. He amasses a mental storehouse of data about dog breeds, delving into the physical and behavioral traits that distinguish one breed from another. Just as he has mastered Disney trivia and animal almanacs, he scrutinizes a dog-breed guide, closely examining what distinguishes, say, a French bulldog from an American bulldog, a cocker spaniel from a springer. Occasionally he accedes to my requests to lead Sasha on walks around the block—the farthest we have ever let Ezra wander without an adult—but he is more enthusiastic about reciting the various categories of canines he has learned from his books: working group, hounds, terriers.

One afternoon we are walking Sasha together when Ezra spots a woman approaching on the sidewalk with a golden retriever.

"Is your dog friendly?" he calls, dashing toward the woman and dropping Sasha's leash, completely forgetting about his own puppy. Sasha, still relatively untrained, begins making for the busy street.

"Ezra!" I call. "Your *dog!*"

I rush to grab Sasha, stopping her flight, but Ezra pays no attention, lost in the retriever.

Our family is attending a crowded picnic concert at a neighborhood park when I realize Ezra has vanished. I stand up and survey the throngs of families lazing on picnic blankets—I have scanned crowds this way so many times in markets and theme parks that my body does it almost instinctively—and finally spot him on a path fifty yards across the park, talking animatedly with a woman who has a smallish brown dog on a leash. Climbing over picnic blankets and around coolers and lawn chairs, I make my way over to him, ready to scold him for dashing away.

"Abba," he says with excitement, ignoring my attempt to admonish him. "She has a Cardigan Welsh corgi!" He tells me he has never seen one before—except in books. "See! The ears are bigger than a Pembroke's."

The woman looks tickled.

"Not many people know the difference," she says.

Ezra does, and the best place to demonstrate that is Rancho Park, just a couple of miles from our home, the place where, years earlier, I noticed dog owners letting their pets run free. We begin visiting, ostensibly to offer

Sasha some exercise, but it is Ezra who discovers his own reason to go: He relishes simply being surrounded by dogs and people who love dogs. Elsewhere, he gets stuck in one-sided conversations focused on the same old topics—Pixar movies, *The Simpsons*—that few others want to discuss at length. Here, though, he has discovered something that changes his life: When he wants to talk endlessly about Burmese mountain dogs and Rhodesian ridgebacks, he is overjoyed to learn that so does everybody else.

Among other twelve-year-olds, gushing about muzzles and cropped tails might render him quirky. At the dog park, it makes him fit right in, delighting owners when he can identify uncommon breeds—the odd Hungarian vizsla, the occasional pharaoh hound—he recognizes from his books.

Just as he is fascinated by humans with unusual physical traits, he is drawn to any dog that looks distinctive—the Chihuahua missing a leg, the bulldog with one eye. When he spots one, he paces around, seeking the human who goes with the dog and then peppering the owner with questions: "How can she walk? . . . What happened to his eye?"

Over time, he becomes familiar not only with the park's canine regulars, but also their human counterparts. Elsewhere, he is isolated, solitary, in his own world. Here he has found a place where he can be part of the pack.

Arriving at the park one afternoon I keep my distance as I watch Ezra and Sasha make their eager sprint into the park. I observe from a distance as my son joins the small cluster of strangers, chatting amiably and gesturing toward the dogs. And I think about the solitary toddler I once knew, gingerly handling toy zebras in the backyard.

"Gosh," one of the women says to me when I catch up with them, "you've got such a social kid."

I smile. Who am I to disagree?

CHAPTER TWELVE

Right and Wrong, Death and God

The brain expands. This is what Ezra's doctor tells us. At an appointment when he is eleven, Shawn mentions that we have started to notice how, in subtle ways, Ezra seems to be more aware of himself than before—perhaps more able to perceive himself in a larger context, in relation to other people. It's as if he has been supernearsighted, a Mr. Magoo walking around in a blur, seeing only what's closest. But now, occasionally he puts on glasses and sees the world clearly. "That's the brain literally growing," Dr. Robinson says. And then she repeats something she has told us before: "When these kids hit adolescence, all bets are off."

Plunging toward the teen years, Ezra is the same boy: the child delighted by animals and cartoons, the kid who can become entangled in his own loops, the young man watching movies in his head. But he is also starting to grapple with larger issues: things like morality, and mortality, and God.

*   *   *

One afternoon, I get a telephone call from Ezra's sixth-grade teacher.

"I just want to make sure you're aware of something," she says. "For the last couple of weeks, Ezra has been buying candy every day at the snack bar."

"You mean with money?" I ask.

"Yes."

"Where did he get the money?"

"I think it's his own. I just wasn't sure whether he had your permission or not, but I thought you should know."

This comes as a shock. Not the candy part: Ezra has long proven adroit at scaring up sources of sugar. Cookies, ice cream, yellow bags of Nestlé chocolate chips all routinely disappear from our kitchen with such consistency that we have often discussed installing locks on the pantry door. What's surprising is that Ezra apparently is using money. We have given him a small allowance, which augments the dollars he collects from the tooth fairy and the occasional birthday check from his grandparents. But he has never demonstrated any understanding of—or even interest in—the mechanics of money. Handling currency is one of those elemental skills that other children pick up intuitively, but to which Ezra seems oblivious. So I had no inkling that my son understood the basic human transaction of exchanging paper bills and silver coins for stuff.

Until now.

Of course, the news is tempered by a troubling detail. Nearly all of Ezra's money is in a bank account.

His younger brother, Noam, on the other hand, is a collector, accumulating Snapple caps, Hot Wheels cars, and my discarded digital watches in plastic bags and shoe boxes stowed in the crevices of his bedroom. All the more so with money, which he methodically socks away, week after week, with vague dreams of a deluxe Lego set or an iPod. He has been resistant to depositing his loot in the bank, preferring to watch the cash accumulate before his eyes.

As soon as I hang up with the teacher, I run upstairs to Noam's room. When I pick up his money jar, I am alarmed to discover only a couple of crumpled dollar bills and a few nickels and pennies where there had been upward of thirty dollars.

My heart sinks: My son is a thief!

My imagination soars: My son understands money!

That afternoon, I'm driving Ezra on an errand, trying to figure out how to broach the subject. Finally, I just ask him.

"Ez, have you been buying candy at school?"

"Yeah, Abba!" he says, not even attempting to hide his excitement. "I can buy M&M's and Oreos at the Snack Shack!" I am struck by his naive sense of enthusiasm and pride. Ezra has no idea that there's anything wrong with this—with pilfering cash, with stealthily obtaining sweets, with hiding all of this from his parents. Or so it appears. Part of me feels irate that a school for children with developmental disabilities doesn't present more of an obstacle between sixth graders and high-fructose corn syrup. Part of me is stuck trying to imagine the scenario.

"How did you get the candy, Ezra?"

"I gave them money!"

"Where did you get the money?"

"From my house."

"Where?"

"From Noam's room," he says evenly.

I pull over to the curb, switch off the ignition, and turn to Ezra, sitting in the backseat.

"You took money from Noam?"

"Don't be mad," he says. "Be happy."

I'm not happy.

"You know what that's called?" I ask.

"Allowance?"

"Do you know what it's called when you take somebody's money?"

Silence.

"Ezra, it's called 'stealing.'"

"Yeah, right! 'Stealing'!" He sounds excited—as if he got a word right in the spelling bee. I have not come with a game plan, but I realize suddenly how important this moment is, this chance to make Ezra recognize the impact of his actions. I have learned over time that the best way to make him understand abstract concepts—like thievery—is to break them down into smaller pieces.

"Ez, do you understand what's wrong with that?"

"I shouldn't *steal*?" he asks.

"Of course you shouldn't steal. Do you know why?"

"I could go to *jail*?"

"Well, yeah," I say. "But what's *wrong* with stealing?"

He has no answer.

"Have you ever heard of the Ten Commandments?" I ask. Ezra attends Hebrew school and he's gone to synagogue nearly every Saturday of his life. His mother is a rabbi. I figure it's a familiar phrase.

"Like, God gave Moses the two tablets at Mount Sinai," he says, launching into the narrative, "and then Moses saw the golden calf and he got very, very angry—"

I interrupt: "Ezra, what are the Ten Commandments?"

He moans, resisting the interrogation, then offers an answer: "What Moses got on the mountain?"

"The Ten Commandments are rules from God. And one of the Ten Commandments says that you should never, ever steal."

"Yeah, right," he says, as if applauding my fine effort. "We shouldn't steal."

"So you broke God's rules."

"Are you *angry*?"

"It's not about my being angry, Ez. When you stole Noam's money, you broke the Ten Commandments."

"They're all broken now?"

The literalist. I try again. "Stealing is against the rules. You're in trouble."

"God's going to *punish* me?"

"No, Ez."

"Do I have to go to *jail*?"

"No, but you need to remember the rules. And there's another reason. What's another bad thing about stealing?"

Silence.

"Does stealing hurt anybody?"

"No . . ." he says tentatively. Then, looking at me: "Yes!"

"Does it?"

"Nnnn—yes?"

"Ezra, whom did you hurt?"

Silence.

"When you took Noam's money, who got hurt?"

I wait. Silence.

"Come on, Ez. You hurt *Noam*!"

"Yeah, *right!*"

"Is that nice?" I ask.

"No, I should not hurt my brother Noam," he says stiffly.

"You shouldn't hurt anybody!" I say. "But when you steal, you hurt people. So what are the reasons not to steal? Number one?"

"Number one: It breaks the Ten Commandments."

"Right," I say. "And number two?"

"It hurts Noam."

"Right—it hurts people. And there's one more reason."

"One more reason," he echoes.

"When you steal, it makes people think bad things about you."

"Yeah, right. People think bad things."

"When you steal, it makes people think, 'That Ezra—he must be a bad person.' Are you a bad person, Ezra?"

"No, of *course* not!"

"What are you?"

"I'm a *good* person."

"So you don't want to steal, or people will think you're a bad person."

We review those three reasons. I drill him until he can recite the breakdown back to me the way he can reel off *Simpsons* characters or lemur subspecies: "It's against the Ten Commandments; it hurts people; it makes people think bad things about me."

After he repeats it a few times, I tell Ezra that I'm proud of him.

"People make mistakes sometimes," I say. "That's how we learn." I start up the car and pull away from the curb, feeling pretty sure I have taught Ezra something he didn't know half an hour earlier.

A few weeks later, Shawn and I receive an e-mail from the teacher. The message: Ezra has spent his lunch hour in detention. The reason: stealing. I get a sinking feeling. The scenario becomes clear: The school uses a behavior-modification system, rewarding good behavior with colored plastic chips that students can accumulate and cash in for prizes at week's end or save for larger rewards. To me, Ezra has seemed oblivious to the entire system. But on this morning, the teacher tells me, my son spotted a container of the chips on the gym teacher's desk—and procured a few handfuls for himself. Chagrined that Ezra has transgressed so soon after the allowance-stealing incident, I am still contemplating how to discipline him when his school bus pulls up to our house that afternoon and Ezra comes barreling through the door.

"Abba!" he says immediately. "Guess what?"

"What, Ez?"

"I broke the Ten Commandments and hurt people and I made people think bad things about me!"

For the moment, I forget about the stealing and the punishment, and savor the realization that my son is developing something new: a conscience.

That same year, he raises the topic of my birthday while we're sharing one of our typed conversations:

"In October, you're going to be 45 years old."

"Yes, I am. I guess I'm getting old."

"No, Abba, not yet. You won't die until you're 60 or 68 years old!"

"You think so? Well, wouldn't that be sad? How would you feel?"

"I would feel sad."

"Who would you go to the zoo with?"

"Ima? No, she doesn't like the reptiles. No, you have to try to not die. Don't eat poison, don't choke, don't get killed, and long live! Don't smoke, drink a lot of milk, do push-ups, and stretch."

It's the beginning of an endless series of conversations about dying. I don't know why Ezra is preoccupied with death—only that he is. Not with the details or the mechanics of dying; not with diseases or murders or funerals. Not suicide. His focus is the statistics: when, how, and who is left behind. To Ezra, it seems, death is another fact for his collection.

I'm writing in my home office early one morning when he's twelve and I hear his distraught voice echoing from the den, where he's on the computer. Seconds later, Ezra appears at my door.

"Bad news, Abba," he says. "Comedian George Carlin dies at seventy-one."

His tone is at once deliberate and flat, like the mechanical corporate phone voice that tells you which number to push for customer service.

I know why Ezra cares about George Carlin. Not because of his famous "Seven Dirty Words" routine or his TV stand-up. Ezra doesn't know about any of that. To him, George Carlin was only one thing: the voice of a Pixar character—Fillmore, the psychedelic VW Microbus in *Cars*, one of Ezra's favorite movies.

"Awww, I'm sorry to hear that, Ez," I say.

"Yeah," says Ezra. "You're very sorry to hear that comedian George Carlin died at seventy-one. That's very sad news."

I follow him as he makes his way back to the computer to keep reading the Pixar blog he scans each morning the way others read box scores or check stock prices. He pauses for a moment, letting the news sink in.

"He died of old age?" he says, more asking than telling.

I answer honestly. "I don't think so," I say. "He was only seventy-one. What does it say?"

Ezra presses his face close to the monitor to read. "'George Carlin died from heart failure,'" he says. Then he looks at me and gets to what this is really about. "Is that going to happen to me?"

Suddenly, all of his Pixar trivia doesn't seem so trivial. Early on a Monday morning, my twelve-year-old son is facing his own mortality.

"Will it, Abba?" he asks again. "Am I going to die from heart failure?"

I put a hand on his shoulder.

"Ez, you'll be okay," I tell him. "Just stay healthy."

"But will I die of heart failure?" he asks.

"God willing, you'll live a long time," I say.

"You're not *sure*?" he asks.

"Ezzy, you will be fine."

This goes on for some time. He starts listing every death he's heard of recently: the family friend who died of leukemia half a year earlier; a friend's elderly father who had succumbed to liver cancer. I imagine Ezra in this new phase, compulsively compiling exhaustive lists like a statistician for the county coroner: who was killed by cancer, who by heart attacks, who by pneumonia. His childlike preoccupations are intersecting with something deep and scary, something all people share: a fear of death.

Just over three months later, we're visiting friends for a weekend lunch when Ezra disappears from the table, then reappears with an announcement.

"More bad news," he says. "Paul Newman is dead at eighty-three."

Around the table, the adults reminisce about Newman's virtuoso performances in films like *Exodus* and *The Verdict*. Ezra is thinking that another *Cars* voice actor has died: the voice of Doc Hudson. For the next several weeks, this is much of what he talks about: If Pixar does a *Cars* sequel, who will do the voices of Fillmore and Doc Hudson? The question occupies his thoughts day and night. He revisits the Pixar blogs daily— several times a day—mostly to find the answer to that question.

"It's unknown," he reports to me. "Who will do the voices of those characters is still unknown."

"Unknown" is a disquieting concept for him. In fact, I suspect that's one of the reasons Ezra has become so focused on death: It's fixed, unchanging, concrete. It's forever. But then there's that other part: the unknown.

In his middle-school social studies classes, he seems incapable of—or uninterested in—grasping much of the curriculum, drowning in a sea of information about historical movements and larger cultural themes. He does, however, remember when the famous people died: Montezuma, 1520. George Washington, 1799. Paul Revere, 1818. World history in Ezra's mind becomes one long parade of dead guys.

Of course, it's not entirely academic. He worries, like anyone else, about the mystery of death. Getting the news that a family friend is in the hospital, he asks immediately: "Did she die?" Even hearing that someone has a common cold induces momentary panic and he asks the same question with which he pesters dog owners. "Is he going to *die* soon?"

Shawn and I can't help but chuckle sometimes at his extreme reactions. We try teaching him to temper his responses: "Of course not, Ezra. It's just a cold." But it's yet another case of Ezra expressing aloud what everyone else is thinking. If we couldn't help it, most of us would spend all day, every day, wondering when our time will be up. We just don't like to think about the unknown.

*   *   *

When your mother is a rabbi, it is difficult to escape the big theological questions that seem to reverberate through the household: Is there a God? Where is God? What does God want from us? What is God? But if Ezra is thinking about any of this, he rarely lets on.

He's just shy of ten. I'm trying to engage him in a typed conversation, but he's mostly begging me to buy a Lego set he knows Noam desperately wants. I try to distract Ezra by asking him about his experience earlier that day in synagogue, where he participated in a service for children with special needs. When he mentions a significant Hebrew prayer, the Shema, I follow up, typing:

"Which part was your favorite?"

"Singing."

"Which prayer did you like singing?"

"Shema."

"Do you know what the Shema means in English?"

"No."

"Do you want to know what it means?"

"Yes. But I want you to let me buy a new Lego Castle of Morcia for Noam on his birthday."

"The Shema means that there is only one God!"

"Yes."

"What is God?"

"God is a big guy."

"What is He like? Or is it She?"

"He is like Moses."

"What kinds of things does God do?"

"God does a lot of things."

"Tell me two things God does."

"No."

"Can you tell me just *one* thing God did?"

"He made the animals."

"Did God make anything else?"

"He made the trees and bees."

"Where can I see God?"

"Everywhere. But please let me buy a new Castle of Morcia for Noam on his birthday."

Beyond that, I don't know whether Ezra thinks much about God. Then, three years later, our family is on a hike in Santa Ynez Canyon, a wooded area not far from the Pacific. When the boys were younger, we returned routinely to this spot, following a gravel-strewn path beside a creek to where it ends at a trickle of a waterfall. Now the boys are older and less compliant. Ezra bounds ahead and I follow. For some reason, he's stuck in a verbal loop talking about Pringles potato chips and cookies.

He's moaning and practically shouting. "I just *love* junk food!" he says. "I'm *obsessing* about junk food."

"So stop," I say. It's not that simple. Ezra seems powerless to extricate himself from his own banter. So as we walk, I spontaneously ask him a question.

"If God could give you anything in the world, what would you want?"

"Junk food," he says.

"I'm serious, Ezzy. If you could have one thing, anything in the world?" And then, I'm not sure why, perhaps inspired by the trees and the creek and the blue sky, I begin talking in the voice of God—or at least the voice of God as heard in *The Ten Commandments*.

"Ezzzzzrrraaaa," I bellow. "I will give you one thing. What do you want?"

I expect him to resist. He is put off by any kind of role-playing games. Usually, his immediate response is to demand, "Stop pretending!" Or simply to moan and cover his ears to demonstrate his frustration and impatience. But this time he does neither; Ezra just keeps walking.

"Would God sound like a male or female?" I ask, back in my own voice.

"Male," he says.

I repeat my question in the divine intonation: "Ezra, if I could give you anything in the world, what would you ask for?"

"A pet," he says quickly.

"Ezra, if you could have *anything* in the world?"

"I would want a frog. A green frog."

"What species?"

"A tree frog."

I'm not sure he understands the game. I try to deepen my voice even lower. "Really? If I could give you *anything* in the world? If you could have a car? Or a trip to Disneyland? Or a house or a big building?"

He changes his mind.

"I would want a car."

"A car? Where would you drive?"

"I would drive around—to synagogue, but not on Shabbat."

"Why not?" I ask, still trying to channel God.

"That's a day when we are happy with what we have and we pray to you," he says, talking to God. Shawn had once explained it to him in exactly those terms as a way to get Ezra to stop focusing on stuff he doesn't have one day a week: God rested on the seventh day, stopped creating the world and just enjoyed what was already there—and he should do the same.

"I like that," I tell him. "That makes me happy. You know why?"

He doesn't say anything.

"Because I rest on Shabbat too!" I say.

We keep walking. Since he is still buying into the God voice, I decide to keep going: "Do you have any questions for me?"

He does: "Do you like being with angels?"

I turn the question back to him: "What are angels?"

"They have wings and they live in heaven."

"Well, I think people can be angels," I tell him, still in the low God voice. "I think people who help you in your life can be angels." I name a few who have helped him.

"Those are people!"

"But I think those people can act like angels." I stay in the God voice. "Do you have any questions about me? Or about you?"

"Why do I ask so many things?" he says. "Ami doesn't do that. Why do I talk about movies so much?"

"Why do you think?" I ask him.

"Because of my brain?" Ezra says.

We're standing by the creek now.

"I can help you to control that," I say. I tell him to put his hands on his head, grasping the sides of his head tightly.

"Repeat after me," I tell him. "'I control my brain—it doesn't control me.'" I have him repeat the phrase a few times. Then I give him a hug.

"Let's keep walking now," he says.

"Any more questions?" I ask.

"Why are you invisible and why can't anyone hide from you?"

I don't have good answers for those. I tell Ezra he's asking good questions and the two of us walk on in silence for a few minutes. I ponder how I got to listen to my son speak to God. And then I notice a small miracle: Ezra has stopped talking about Pringles.

CHAPTER THIRTEEN

Three Questions

I'm at Starbucks with a friend talking about work and friends and children when suddenly she wants to know how Ezra's mind works. She begins rattling off questions about school and memory and behavior and consciousness.

"Do you mind my asking?" she says.

"No, it's fine," I tell her. Some people we know step gingerly on the topic. Some avoid it. Some say whatever comes to mind.

"I mean, will he grow out of it? Will he grow up and be normal?"

I take a sip of my latte and think about *normal*. What is normal, anyway? And when is anyone grown up? And do I know what *anyone* will be like in five or ten or twenty years?

As Ezra's father, I often find myself in the position of trying to explain him—to friends or relatives or, sometimes, strangers, like the clerk at PETCO who watches him stand for thirty or forty minutes with his nose pressed up against the Plexiglas of the mouse cage, watching the tiny creatures swarm around the hamster wheel. The clerk, wearing a red vest and carrying a broom, finally speaks up.

"Is it autism?" he asks.

I nod.

"What kind?"

Over time, my answers have evolved, but the questions have remained consistent. Most people who meet Ezra or who know something about him have variations on the same three questions:

Does he know he's different?

How do his brothers deal with it?

What's his future?

This is how Ezra learns that he has something called autism. We have never hidden it from him. He has sat at the dinner table (or paced around it) for years while we have discussed the topic. He has been to countless appointments with therapists and doctors when Shawn and I have discussed him and his challenges. Often, I have wondered how much he understands what we are talking about. At times I have assumed that he comprehends, but cannot express it. On other occasions, I have been fairly sure he was lost in his own thoughts, and simply not paying attention. Around the time he is twelve, Ezra begins to gain a semblance of self-awareness, perhaps begins noticing in subtle ways that he is unique.

We are on the Oregon coast, where my parents own a vacation home, a compact, geometric structure that perches over the Pacific on a stretch of beach populated by only a couple of hundred homes. Nearly every summer, we make the pilgrimage here, usually with extended family, to relax in the fresh air, stroll on the wide beaches, read novels, and watch the waves. When the boys were younger, Ami and Noam would spend long hours constructing elaborate systems of canals in the sand to channel the water from a creek that runs into the ocean just adjacent to the house. While they labored in collaboration with a few cousins and my brothers, Ezra would sit alone not far away, tossing fist-size stones into the creek, one after another, and listening to them hit water: *plop, plop, plop*. He did that for hours, a small boy lost in the addictive, repetitive rhythms of grabbing, tossing, listening, and tossing again.

On this day, he is alone in a different way. My parents have joined us for the weekend, and so have the families of both of my brothers. It's an informal family reunion. By night we gather for large, communal dinners. By day, the sixteen of us (septuagenarians through toddlers) spread out in many directions—some jogging, some digging, some reading—except for one breezy Saturday afternoon when the whole group joins on a stretch of beach for a spontaneous game of kickball. Everyone, that is, except for Ezra, who gets shuffled onto a team, but seems less than enthused about it. He has never shown a hint of interest in team sports. (A single season on a T-ball team proved bewildering, as the rules seemed to defy his grasp and he showed up mostly to earn the postgame snacks of granola bars or Cheetos.) I'm on his team and I try to direct him as we spread out across the makeshift field, but after a short time, he grows defiant and cranky, marching off, arms folded, and collapses into the soft sand nearby. The game proceeds and he remains by himself. As I glance up at him from the game, it strikes me: Even here, among the people who love him most in the world, Ezra is alone.

I keep playing, but Shawn heads over to try retrieving him. He resists, striding with conviction toward the creek to throw his beloved stones.

"Come on, Ezzy!" I can hear her calling after him. "Everybody is here. We want you with us."

Ezra silently folds his arms across his chest again, resisting his mother's appeals with dramatic flair. She approaches him and he dashes farther away. From my place in the kickball game, I can see my wife chasing my son in crazy, pell-mell circles on the beach. Finally she catches him, throws an arm around his shoulders, and the two of them walk back to a spot a bit down the beach, where together they sink into the sand and sit side by side watching the waves and feeling the wind on their faces. I keep playing, my mind only half in the game, wondering how she will get him back.

She doesn't. They get up and walk down the beach together, and I don't see them until later, when the game is over and the cousins have dispersed across the beach and back toward the house.

"I told him," Shawn tells me.

"You told him . . ." I say, raising my eyebrows, wondering what she means.

"I told him he has autism," Shawn says. "We had the talk."

For a moment I am stunned—not in a good way. Usually, Shawn and I are in sync on such matters. We have talked and theorized and even consulted with professionals about the appropriate time to explain Ezra's diagnosis to him directly. As usual, I'm the one who delays the decision, weighing, researching, and waiting. Shawn is more intuitive.

"I'm sorry," she says, seeing my puzzled expression. "I know we should have discussed it."

"I assumed we would. . . ."

"I'm sorry," she repeats. "It was just the moment to do it."

I forgive her. "Did he get it?" I ask.

"I think so."

"What did you tell him?" I ask.

Shawn recounts the conversation as it started, with her calling after him to rejoin the family.

"Why do I have to?" Ezra had responded.

"Because we're all together and you're part of the family," Shawn had told him.

Ezra kept walking, picking up the pace and forcing Shawn to follow in pursuit.

"Come on; Ami and Noam are there," Shawn said.

"But I'm different from Ami and Noam," he said.

Shawn caught up to him and paused by his side.

"I'm not different?" he asked, backtracking.

"Do you *feel* different?"

"I'm different because I don't go to the same school," he said. "Three brothers can't go to the same school? That would be against the rules?" As was his habit, he turned each sentence into a question.

"No, you *could* go to the same school, but you go to a school that's better for you."

"I'm not the same as Ami and Noam?"

"You're not," Shawn finally answered. Since he had broached the topic, she told me later, she decided to follow his lead. When she and I had discussed this very revelation with various professionals over the years, most agreed that there was no correct time to explain a diagnosis to a child. They did warn that for the child, the revelation is often followed by a period of depression—sadness that comes from the prospect of going through life never fitting in. Ezra, for all of his quirks and challenges, had always been at heart a happy person, and I dreaded seeing that cheerful essence shattered.

"Do you know what makes you different?" Shawn asked.

"I'm a different age?"

"That's true, Ezra, but you're also different because you have something called autism." She paused and let that sink in. He didn't respond. "Have you heard that word?"

He shook his head. We had used the word in conversations probably thousands of times over the years when he was present (physically, at least).

"Autism means your brain works a little bit differently from other people's." Ezra listened. "Autism is why you have such a great memory and you know so many things about animals and movies."

"It means I'm smart?"

"You are very smart, sweetie. But sometimes it also makes it hard. You know how sometimes you repeat things a lot? And it can make it hard to play with other kids."

"It's bad?" Ezra asked. He was working so hard to understand.

Shawn shook her head. "No, sweetie. It's not bad. It's just part of you."

"Aut—what's it called?"

"Autism, sweetheart."

"Autism is good?" he asked.

"Do you think so?" Shawn asked.

He smiled. "Yeah. It's good."

"I think it's *very* good, because it makes you the Ezra that Ima and Abba love."

"Yeah!" Ezra said, brightening. "Autism is good!"

"Do you want to ask any questions about it?" Shawn asked.

"No! Autism is good!" was all he said.

"You know what?"

"What?"

"We love you very, very much and we're very proud of you."

"Yeah, you're proud of me," he repeated. He leaped to his feet. "Yeah!" he shouted as the wind blew and they made their way back toward the house. "I have autism and I'm smart!"

I entered parenthood knowing nothing about neurological disorders, but with a PhD's worth of wisdom about another condition Ezra had been dealt, through no fault of his own: He was the middle of three sons. So was I, and growing up with a brother two years my senior and another three years younger had left its scars from battles over things like bedroom turf, vinyl LPs, and parental attention. I knew what it was like to be neither the esteemed oldest child nor the coddled youngest, to be just, as I was known in my family, Tom in the middle. It meant that I could fall victim to an older brother who, at times, punched my shoulder at will, but then face certain punishment when I attempted to deliver the same tough love to my younger sibling. Of course, things improved as the three of us grew older, and the fluke of birth order placed me at the center of a nurturing family that sustained me into adulthood.

For Ezra, being the middle son is a mixed blessing. He has little social impulse and a tendency to operate in isolation, but his place in the family forces him to live in constant interaction with other human beings. As he fights his own turf wars over computer time and chocolate-chip cookies—the way any sibling does—Ezra by necessity learns to exert himself, engage in internecine combat, and constantly contemplate the motives and desires of the other boys. At school he can choose to operate in his own sphere; at the zoo he can wander in isolation; but at home, Ezra has no choice but to forge bonds.

Early on, we struggle with how and when to explain to Ami—two years older—the nature of his brother's diagnosis. In our attempts to be sensitive and enlightened, it turns out that we aren't unlike parents who fret over teaching Johnny about sex, only to discover that he has mastered the subject already at summer camp or on the school bus.

When Ezra is four and Ami is six, we begin attending a weekly support group for families of children with diagnoses similar to Ezra's. Every Wednesday afternoon, I meet Shawn and our three sons at a church social hall, where a therapist with expertise in autism leads a discussion group for parents over a long conference table, while nearby, young adults supervise Ezra and his peers in one room, and their siblings—clustered by age—separately. Neophytes as special-needs parents, Shawn and I have both found value in the discussions, which mix emotional support with practical advice ("remove labels from new shirts—they drive the kids crazy"). It is the first time the two of us are meeting other parents of children like Ezra, and I find it comforting and encouraging—and occasionally frightening—to share time with others experiencing the same journey.

As much as we derive strength and fellowship there, we have never explained to any of the boys why, exactly, our family is participating in the program. We refer to the weekly meeting as simply "playgroup." I wonder at times whether Ami has noticed that a disproportionate number of children in Ezra's group are boys who spend the hour flapping their arms or spinning in circles instead of, say, playing Parcheesi. The question never comes up, and as far as I know, he considers playgroup just another family activity, along the lines of synagogue services or his soccer league.

One week, the five of us have just piled into Shawn's minivan after the weekly meeting when Ami speaks up from the back row with a question.

"What's autism?"

Shawn and I share a glance and I take a deep breath and let it out slowly.

"Why are you asking?" she says.

"Jennifer had us all go around and answer questions," he says. "And then she said, 'Now try answering the way your sibling with autism would answer.'"

I feel a surge of anger and frustration. How could the group leader have been so injudicious? How could she have broached that topic without checking first with the parents? I feel violated, like something precious we have been guarding has been destroyed. Shawn and I were offered no choice, no chance to discuss the matter, and now we have to muddle through the aftermath.

Then again, who am I fooling? Ami is an intelligent and sensitive little boy. For all of our attempts at euphemism, it *is* a program for families coping with autism. Maybe what pains me so much isn't Jennifer's slip, but something else. Maybe what I feel is sadness that Ami's relationship with his brother will never be the same; that the idiosyncratic kid who shares his bedroom—the one who dumps toys instead of playing with them, the one who incessantly asks him if videos are "for big kids or little kids"—is now somebody else: his "sibling with autism."

That evening, Shawn and I take some time to sit with Ami and explain the term, being careful to keep the description positive—or at least neutral: This is the way God created Ezra, and there is nothing wrong with it; it's just the way he is. Ami looks back and forth at the two of us as we go to pains to couch the information—what little we understand then ourselves—in the least painful way possible, forgetting, perhaps, that he has watched us struggle with this for a couple of years.

"I knew all that," he finally says when we pause. "I just didn't know that word."

Once he does, he embraces it. When they were both toddlers—before Ezra's diagnosis, or any inkling of it—Shawn worried aloud that our two oldest children didn't seem to play together with the kind of natural chemistry she had seen in other pairs of young siblings.

"They will," I assured her. "Just give it some time."

But as they grew, they only became more different. Practically from birth, Ami cheerfully socialized with adults and peers alike. Even in our house, he constantly seeks out company and connection. When he learns to play guitar, instead of holing up in his bedroom, he seeks out Shawn and me to demonstrate a new chord he picked up or a song he has mastered. Where Ezra lacks any impulse to interact with most people, his older brother rarely prefers to be alone. Despite the gulf between them, Ami seldom expresses anger, or even regret, about Ezra. They don't fight; they don't play. They coexist, with little in common but genuine caring. Ami doesn't naturally gravitate to Ezra as a companion, but he looks out for him, sharing his own friends with him, and in some ways understands him better than anyone.

When Ami is twelve, the organizers of an educators' conference invite him to speak on a panel. The topic: siblings of special-needs children. Shawn and I watch from the back of the room as Ami ably fields question after question from the sixty or so professionals, all the while exuding a kind of sweet nonchalance, as if the entire topic is of little consequence.

"He's just a person," he says of his middle brother. "He's a little unusual, but the way I see it, he's just another kid."

Noam's relationship with Ezra is more complex. Just under two years younger, Noam was still an infant when Ezra began veering off course, and for a time, the two boys are nearly constant playmates, Noam trailing after Ezra, imitating or joining his every movement, however wild or irrational. If Ezra dumps a box of wooden blocks, Noam dumps one too. If Ezra swings at high speeds on the backyard swing set, Noam joins him with pleasure.

When they are five and three, Shawn travels for several days to New York. Ezra, on one of his routine search-and-destroy missions through the house, somehow breaks into a box of her tampons, opening two dozen one by one and laying them out across the carpet outside the bathroom. Pleased with his brother's handiwork, Noam runs to alert me.

"Look, Abba! Ima's going to be so happy!" he says. "Ezra found her candles!"

We develop a tongue-in-cheek title for him: Ezra's best therapist. When nobody else knows what to do with our middle son, when I run out of patience, when Ezra flees contact and runs out the back door into chilly winter mornings in only his underwear, Noam plays with him, undeterred. He has an essential kindness, and doesn't have a fixed idea of what an older brother is supposed to act like—or realize that most of them don't incessantly repeat bits of dialogue from *Veggie Tales* and flap their arms like birds. Noam spins around like Ezra, rolls in blankets with him, watches his videos, and joins in his silly revelry.

Shawn and I both know it will end someday—that Noam will pass Ezra by. One day Noam will tire of the swinging and the blankets and the zoo visits and want to move on and do what most boys do at five or six or seven: Little League, karate class, video games.

A therapist tells us that siblings of children with diagnoses like Ezra's often react with anger—at first subconscious, then more overt. At six, all Noam wants is for the world to make sense. That logical universe doesn't have much room for an older brother who acts like a younger brother, so Noam does occasionally display frustration beyond the typical sibling conflict. It is lucky for Ezra that these subtle nuances of the social world pass him by like helium balloons floating past. He doesn't seem troubled as his younger brother slowly loses interest in most of the things he so loves—otters, Disney movies, juvenile games—and moves on to his own passionate pursuits: violin, origami, and a growing circle of close friends. The two still occasionally play Wii games together or giggle over a YouTube video of a cat. It's different, but a reminder of the bond they share. Increasingly, they get into little tiffs—just the kind of squabbles I had with my own brothers.

One summer afternoon when Ezra and Noam, twelve and ten, are at sleepaway camp, I receive a phone call from Tova, a counselor who has known them both for years.

"It's about Ezra and Noam," she says. At first I'm concerned—such calls are rare—but then she explains. "I just spotted the sweetest thing— they were off together, just the two of them, hunting for frogs," she says. "I just thought a parent would want to know."

I smile, grateful for small moments.

In a cabinet in our bedroom, Shawn and I keep our family memorabilia: finger-painted Mother's Day cards the boys created in kindergarten; summer camp group portraits, shoe boxes stuffed with photos from the early years, back when you got two sets of prints in a yellow envelope with your negative strips. Toward the back of a deep, cluttered shelf sits one box I have rarely touched: a plastic bin stuffed with videotapes we shot in the first years of our children's lives. With our busy schedules working and coordinating three children's packed days and weeks, we rarely have a moment to indulge in watching nostalgic footage. There is another reason—an unspoken one—we haven't ventured into the video box: We both know that before he was two and a half, that rocky season when he began lining up plastic animals and overnight seemed to become lost in his own thoughts, Ezra's development had been more or less normal. I didn't articulate it, even to myself, but I was not sure I ever wanted to see the Ezra of six months or a year before that, the preautism Ezra.

One summer day, when all three children are away at camp, Shawn, missing her sons, gets a hankering to peek at the videos. I resist, though my hesitation is tempered by curiosity, so I retrieve the bin and the two of us sit on the carpeted den floor, sifting through the miniature videotapes, most of them untagged.

I find one with my handwriting on the label: "Ezra's bris." I pause a moment, shrugging in reluctance, then insert the tape into the player.

The blurry, poorly lit images show a crowd gathered in our rented apartment in Manhattan for the ceremony marking Ezra's circumcision. It's January of 1996. Chilly winter sunlight streams into the windows. I'm wearing a suit and a tallit, a prayer shawl; Shawn, a black dress with small white polka dots. A babysitter holds Ami, at twenty months, a grinning, blond, wide-eyed ray of sunshine. I see our four parents—in their late fifties, looking fit and happy, clearly buoyed by the celebration of a new grandchild. We fast forward through most of the ritual, except for a few seconds when, with baby Ezra crying just after the circumcision, the camera focuses on Shawn, sitting out of view of the baby, listening to her newborn's sobs, wiping a tear, then closing her eyes in contemplation. I wonder what she is thinking at that moment, what hopes and dreams she holds for this tiny boy with his thick head of black hair.

We watch our younger selves explaining his name: Ezra Moshe, for two of his great-grandfathers. Shawn is congested, and still recovering from her four hours in the operating room a week earlier. I sound eager and upbeat and maybe a bit naive when I express our wishes for our new son.

The rabbi shares a Jewish teaching on the importance of names: the one parents give, the one a person is known by, "and most of all the name he will make for himself with his own life."

"Seen enough?" I ask Shawn in the den.

She grins. "Let's look at another."

I pop in a tape that turns out to be from two years later. Shawn is pregnant, weeks away from delivering Noam. The camera follows Ami—nearly four and endlessly loquacious—and Ezra—brown eyes, long, gorgeous lashes, playfully eating a slice of cheese pizza about half the size of his body. Then he wanders about his bedroom, holding on to a hunk of red Play-Doh and mugging for the camera. That scene ends abruptly and then Ami and Ezra are in the bathtub splashing each other, talking, singing. Off camera, I'm ticking off names of relatives, waiting for Ezra to complete the pairs.

"Bubbe and . . ." I say.

"Grandpa!" he says.

"Shana and . . ."

"Alex!" he says, naming a cousin.

In the den, I scoot my body closer to the wide-screen television, looking closely to see if I can detect a sign of anything amiss, but all I see is a nearly two-year-old little boy—sly, charming, sweet, engaged, looking straight back at the camera, directly at me.

As we watch, I reach out and squeeze Shawn's hand. Neither of us says anything. There's nothing to say. It's like watching a Hitchcock movie, where the suspense lies in the audience knowing what the characters on-screen haven't figured out yet: what's going to happen next.

But in real life, you can't predict the future. You just never know. In later years—long after the bris, the bath, the diagnosis—people who know Ezra will occasionally ask me what his life will look like when he's an adult.

The question can come in the most awkward ways. When Ezra is nine and we are in the midst of our home renovation, I run into Doug, a neighbor, who inquires about progress on the project.

"So," he asks, "are you guys going to add a wing with a bathroom for Ezra?"

I'm not sure I have understood the question correctly. I tell Doug that there will be a lavatory for the three boys to share.

"But I mean, you've got to think about down the line," he says, "when he's going to be living with you as an adult."

Ezra is nine. Every year since his diagnosis, he has grown and progressed in ways that have exceeded most of our expectations and left me in awe of the new aspects of himself he has revealed: his remarkable memory, his growing self-awareness, his sense of humor. I have never considered that he might spend his adult years under our roof. Doug, who hardly knows him, has put limitations on my son. But I see the future as an open question.

I once ask Dr. Robinson, Ezra's autism specialist, whether our son might ever earn a driver's license. It has struck me how much difficulty he has with ordinary judgments and coordination, and I wonder what the chances are that he might overcome those challenges enough to drive a car. I picture him at twenty or thirty, alone, riding the big blue buses I see roaring by on Pico Boulevard, gazing out the window at the movie billboards passing by.

"Will he go to college? Probably," Dr. Robinson says. "Will he have a job? I think so. Will he drive?" She pauses. "My patients surprise me all the time."

For his part, Ezra has never liked talking about the distant future. It's not unusual for adults to ask children what they want to do when they grow up. Seeing his interest in animals or his passion for animation, acquaintances frequently ask him if he might like to become a veterinarian, say, or an artist. As early as ten or eleven, he devises his standard response—one that sounds uncharacteristically mature. "Right now," he says, "I just want to focus on my childhood."

The unknown has always been what Ezra fears the most—who doesn't?—and this is his way of protecting himself from having to think too much about it.

One Thursday a few weeks before his bar mitzvah, I pick up Ezra from Hebrew school. He takes part once a week at our synagogue's after-school program, and rarely chooses to share much about the experience with me. I ask anyway.

"We made a frame," he tells me. The class has been studying the traditions surrounding Jewish weddings. As an art project, each student has decorated a picture frame meant for photos. As he decorated, he tells me, he painted words.

"I didn't write 'wedding,'" he says.

"What do you mean?" I ask.

"I just wrote 'born—bar mitzvah—blank,'" Ezra says.

"What do you mean?"

"On the frame, there were three spaces. I wrote 'born: January nineteenth, 1996. Bar mitzvah: April twenty-fifth, 2009. Wedding: blank.'"

I think I understand.

"Do you think you'll get married?" I ask.

"Of *course* I will," Ezra says.

"Who will you marry?"

Silence. At thirteen, Ezra has never had a close friend. At least, not a peer his own age. But he is certain he'll get married. I feel gratified by his healthy sense of optimism.

"Whoever marries you," I say, "will have to be really interested in . . ."

". . . in me?" he interrupts.

"Well, yeah. But I was going to say she'll have to be really interested in Pixar movies."

Silence.

"Because you are."

Silence.

"You think you can find someone like that?"

He starts to get agitated, the way he does when things take a turn he wasn't expecting and he feels out of control.

"Let's talk about this another time," Ezra says.

We drive home, and I look in the rearview mirror at my son, sitting in the same seat in the car where he has sat as we have shared so many conversations. And for right now, I try to focus on his childhood.

CHAPTER FOURTEEN

Remembering the Future

Seven days before his bar mitzvah, Ezra is stuck.

It's not the Hebrew prayers he will have to recite that are bothering him; after many months of hard work, he knows those. It isn't the *d'var Torah*, the speech he will be delivering, that's causing the problem. That, after considerable struggle, is under control. It is not the sizable crowd of relatives and friends we are anticipating; such things don't make Ezra nervous. It isn't the party or the packed schedule of events at which he, as the guest of honor, will be expected to greet and mingle, hug and kiss. Much of that is still difficult to imagine, but that isn't the problem.

It's the gifts.

The envelopes begin arriving in late March, a couple of months after Ezra turns thirteen and a full month before the event. Each weekday afternoon, he hops off the school bus, sprints up the walk, bursts through the front door, drops his red backpack on the foyer's hardwood floor, and dashes to the mail table.

"Anything for me?" he asks, flipping through the day's mail and tossing to the floor clothing catalogs, credit card offers, and the gas bill.

"Over there," I say, pointing to a couple of pastel envelopes with handwritten addresses.

"For *me*! Ezra!" he cries, grabbing them and tearing open the first envelope—literally ripping it, with such force and speed that in the process he severs a corner of the card.

"Slow down!" I say. "Let's see who it's from!"

He ignores me, intent on reaching the guts of the package, but I seize the shredded envelope from his hands and hold it at arm's length, out of his reach, while I snatch the second envelope with my other hand.

"Give it back! Give it *baaaack*!" Ezra shouts, lunging toward me.

"Slow *down*, Ez!" I say. "Let's sit down with these."

He protests with a groan, but I point to the brown living room couch nearby, and he plunks his body next to mine, reaching and clawing for the envelope.

"*Give* it to me!"

I grab his wrist. "Stop!" He is slipping into tantrum mode. "Take a deep breath, Ezzy."

He does—not slowly, but grabbing two rushed gasps, like he is hyperventilating.

"Give it to me!" he repeats, and I wonder what the point is of trying to slow him down when it seems such torture to him, like waving a chocolate-chip cookie in front of him and telling him he needs to wait. I want him to take in each gift, each sweet note written in longhand by some generous loved one—an aunt or uncle, a teacher or family friend. I want him to comprehend and absorb who sent the gift, to understand that it came with affection and care. I want Ezra to grasp that he is surrounded by love.

He wants the loot.

"All right, Abba! Let me *open* it!"

"Will you slow down?"

"Yes!"

I hand him the torn card. He reads the note, not the handwritten message, but the Hallmark inscription—"'On this special day in your life . . .'"—in a singsong voice, skipping words here and there in his rush.

"Who's it from?" I ask.

Struggling to make out the handwriting, he reads the name, then grabs the check.

"Fifty-four dollars!" Ezra says with exuberance. "Am I rich yet?" The checks always come in multiples of eighteen. *Chai*, the Hebrew word for "life," has a numerical value of eighteen. When I celebrated my own bar mitzvah in 1975, the checks were for eighteen dollars. One family sent a card with a sketch of the Western Wall in Jerusalem and, inside, eighteen crisp one-dollar bills. Nobody sends Ezra eighteen dollars. The cards still have the same picture of the Western Wall, but the givers have adjusted for inflation: The checks are for thirty-six or fifty-four or even a hundred and eighty dollars. Is he rich yet?

"You're getting there," I say. He has already fled to play on the computer, leaving me with shredded pieces of the envelope, the card, and fifty-four dollars from the Shapiros.

The checks seem hardly to enter his consciousness, but after a few weeks of this, Ezra has discovered the magical power of asking. When relatives and friends began inquiring months before about what might be an appropriate bar mitzvah gift for Ezra, Shawn and I conferred with him and began compiling a list. Ami at that age favored an iPod, baseball memorabilia, and contributions toward a laptop. Ezra has specific and unique requests: a new three-volume *Star Wars* encyclopedia he read about on the Internet; a thick, pricey illustrated Disney treasury he spotted at a bookstore years earlier. Mostly, though, he is fixated on gift cards from some of his favorite stores, places like Borders and Target and Barnes & Noble. He doesn't have plans for spending them; he simply likes the idea of the shiny plastic cards.

I should have known that giving Ezra free rein to request gifts might prove hazardous. Shawn and I have learned over the years to cope with his unusual fixations at birthday time by limiting his wish lists to a few requests, and then making sure that every item ends up in one of the wrapped packages when the day comes. What Ezra doesn't like is surprises. He possesses a deep need to know what gifts will be arriving, as if he's a bingo player waiting for the announcer to call out his numbers. As excited as he is each day anticipating the mail, it makes him more and more nervous and agitated when the exact gifts he has requested don't arrive.

That's where he is stuck. The whole process has triggered an entirely new set of anxieties. A psychologist might surmise that he has channeled his angst about something else—the bar mitzvah service, say, or facing adolescence—into his fixation on the presents. But I know Ezra well enough to understand his priorities. It's about the gifts.

"Will I get the *Star Wars Encyclopedia*?" he keeps asking.

"I don't know."

"But will I get it?"

"If you don't, you can use one of your gift cards to buy it yourself."

"I might not *get* it?"

"I'm not sure."

Panicked: "I might not *get* it?"

"I hope so. I don't know."

Those three words—*I don't know*—are so painful to a boy who thrives on the predictable and fixed that they send him into endless cycles of panicked questioning. In the weeks leading up to his bar mitzvah, while Shawn and I are preoccupied with catering menus, centerpieces, and errands to make sure all three boys have the outfits they need, we live with an endless litany of Ezra's repeated questions about gift cards and books and what the next day's mail might bring.

And now he is stuck. I'm not sure what has triggered his reaction. Perhaps it was the generous family friend who, with the best of intentions, ordered the single-volume *Star Wars* book Ezra already owned instead of the 1,190-page, three-volume encyclopedia he was dreaming about. She might as well have sent a box of Brillo pads.

"That's not what I *wanted*!" he cries. "I already *have Star Wars: The Ultimate Visual Guide*!"

"Don't worry. We can exchange it," I assure him. Trying to explain the intricacies of Amazon's return policy at that moment is like attempting to educate a toddler whose balloon has flown away about the chemical properties of helium.

"But I will get *The Complete Star Wars Encyclopedia*."

"Yes."

"I *will*."

"Yes."

"Of course I will get that book."

The verbal looping continues for hours. He is thirteen years old, a lanky teenager with early acne and an unkempt head of brown hair, but he can back himself into the same kind of dead end as when he was a toddler, endlessly reciting lines from *Winnie the Pooh* or, a few years later, incessantly asking people if they were Jewish or Christian.

Something about that bothers me deeply. We are expending much thought, energy, and money to mark his passage toward adulthood, but in significant ways, my middle son is no different from the little boy who seemed so remote and difficult to reach.

That painful truth also strikes me the evening I take Ezra shopping for some dress clothes for the bar mitzvah weekend. Fully into puberty, he has entered that adolescent shopping territory: too big for the children's department, too small for the men's section. The two of us make our way up a pair of escalators to the third floor of the Nordstrom store, where a perky young woman in Baby and Kids introduces herself as Jessica.

"Let me know if there's anything I can do to help," she says. I smile and ask where the blazers are.

"For him?" she says, sizing up Ezra, whose last twelve months have been one continual growth spurt. A full head taller than Jessica, Ezra stares away into the distance, twitching slightly and bouncing on the balls of his feet. The boy never stands still.

Certainly not here on the third floor of Nordstrom. Jessica—cute, energetic, her hair pulled back neatly to achieve the tidy, polished look that all Nordstrom clerks have—surveys a rack of blue jackets. She grabs one, then turns back toward us to hold it up to his body. "He looks like a twenty long. . . ."

Ezra is gone. Jessica smiles. She has been in Baby and Kids long enough to be unfazed by peripatetic children. I glance through the department, past toddler-size shoes and frilly dresses and the glass cases of miniature neckties, trying to spot my son.

"Hang on a sec," I say, dashing to catch him.

Near the cashier station, I find Ezra. He is lying on his belly on the carpeted floor, examining a low shelf of stuffed bears.

"Ezra! Come on! We're trying on jackets!"

"I want to see the bears," he says.

"Later. Come *on*."

Grasping both his hands with mine, I pull him to his feet and back over toward the blazers, helping him awkwardly struggle into the one Jessica has picked out. Close enough.

"Do you want to look at some shirts?" she asks.

Jessica points to the shelf and I pluck out a pair of white button-downs and lead Ezra toward the dressing room. Jessica unlocks a door and I follow Ezra in. He sits down on the floor. He doesn't understand why we are here. This is part of Ezra: He experiences every new situation as a mystery. What might seem natural and ordinary to others—to select pieces of clothing and enter a changing room to test the fit—to him is like landing in a foreign country. Or on the moon. I know what he is thinking: *Why are we in this tiny room? Why does my dad have those clothes? Who was that woman? And why is she waiting outside the door and asking us if we're all right?*

I tell him to take off his shirt, so he can try on the button-down. He slips off his T-shirt as I quickly pull what seem like fifteen or twenty straight pins from the shirt's crevices and remove the cardboard and tissue. When I look up, Ezra is staring intently into the full-length mirror, examining his image. Shirtless, he leans close to the glass, gazing into his own eyes, giggling and mumbling something I can't hear. Mesmerized by his own reflection, he slowly begins licking the mirror.

"Ezra!" I say. "Stop!"

I hand him the shirt. He begins trying it on, backward, the way I remember wearing smocks made from my father's discarded dress shirts in kindergarten.

Then I hear Jessica outside the dressing room.

"Everything going okay?"

That Saturday afternoon, I decide to take Ezra out for some air. Earlier in the day, he had been repeatedly inquiring about the *Star Wars* encyclopedia and the gift cards, again and again begging for assurance that his requested items would arrive soon. When his nonstop imploring spills into the afternoon, I know I need to do something to help him out of his mental jam.

"Come on," I finally tell him. "We're going for a walk."

I grab Sasha's leash, clip it onto her collar, and the two of us head out the door. Ezra and I routinely take these weekend afternoon walks. Before we acquired Sasha we called them our "dog walks," because Ezra would seek out dogs in the neighborhood, barraging their owners with questions and kneeling to greet the animals face-to-face. Now that we have our own dog, I use it as an excuse to get Ezra out to walk around the neighborhood. Even as we walk, he continues his jabber. "Will I get the *Complete Star Wars Encyclopedia,* Abba? . . . I'll get more Borders gift cards? . . . But I will get *The Complete Star Wars Encyclopedia!*"

I finally stop him: "Why do you keep asking?"

"I want to be *sure.*"

"But I have told you hundreds of times."

"You're *mad* at me?"

"Do I look mad?" He stops walking and examines my face earnestly to see if my expression might yield a clue.

"No . . . you're not *mad!*" he says, as much to himself as to me.

"I'm not angry," I say. Sasha is pulling on the leash, so we continue strolling. "I am just frustrated."

"You're frustrated?"

"I'm worried because you won't stop talking about presents."

"I'm *obsessing*?" He knows he is. It is only in the last year or so that he has come to understand terms like *obsessing*. Somehow, that doesn't stop the obsessing.

"I feel like you're stuck."

Ezra looks down: guilty as charged.

"Yeah, I'm stuck," he says quietly.

"I'm concerned," I say, "because how many bar mitzvahs are you going to have in your life?"

He does not answer.

"How many, Ez?"

"One."

"That's right. You only get one. It should be one of the greatest days of your life. So many people who love you are coming to be with you. And they're all excited to see you and talk to you."

"Yeah," he says.

"But Ima and I are worried that you won't be able to enjoy it." I put some force and volume into my voice to be sure I am getting through. "We're worried that you will be so stuck thinking about presents that you'll miss the day. Your bar mitzvah will come and go and all you'll be thinking about will be the *Star Wars* encyclopedia and the Looney Tunes DVD."

I look at him, worried that my invoking the gifts will ignite his rant all over again. Ezra is quiet a moment, seeming to give ear.

"I shouldn't talk about those gifts?"

"No. You need to stop."

"But I *can't* stop," he says, pleading. He is nearly sobbing—more from frustration with his own mind than with me. "I really *want* those presents!"

We have turned onto Beverly Drive, the tree-lined main artery of our neighborhood. We stop on the sidewalk, and Sasha sits on a grassy median strip next to the trunk of a bushy ficus tree. On the spot, I come up with a plan for Ezra.

"I want you to take all those thoughts about presents, okay? And put them all into one place in your brain."

He seems to be listening.

"Every thought you have about the *Star Wars* book or the gift cards or the DVDs, put them all into a black lump inside your brain."

"But I . . ."

I hold up a hand. "Don't say anything! Did you put all those thoughts in a lump?"

"Yes."

"Do you have them all in one place?"

"Yes."

"Did you forget any?"

"No."

"Now I want you to take that lump and pull it out of your brain, and out through your ear." I cock my head as if I were doing it myself.

"You're pretending?" Ezra asks.

"No, I'm serious. Take it out of your brain."

Ezra follows me, tilting his head and miming the actions of extracting something from his ear. He makes a fist with his right hand.

"Do you have the lump in your hand?"

"Yes."

"Is it all there?"

"Yes!"

"Okay, now, you see that tree over there?" I point at another large ficus, directly across Beverly.

"That one?"

"No—that one, on the left."

"Yeah."

"We're going to throw the black lump over there."

"There's not really a—"

"Yes." I ignore him. "Throw it over there—ready? One, two . . ."

Ezra stretches his right hand back, and then extends it forward, pretending to throw. He keeps his eyes on the tree, as if waiting for something to happen.

I put my arm around him. "See it over there?"

"Yes."

"Okay, we're going to leave it there. We're not going to think about gifts all week. They're all under that tree on Beverly Drive."

"But—"

"Whenever you start to think about those presents you want, put those thoughts under the tree on Beverly Drive. And if you can do that, then we'll come back next Sunday, the day after your bar mitzvah, and we'll dig up that lump, and then we can talk about gifts again."

"Okay."

"Are you leaving it there?"

"Yes."

"When will we get it?" I ask.

"Next Sunday, the day after my bar mitzvah."

"Right!"

I take my son's hand and we walk toward home.

What will Ezra's bar mitzvah look like? Our family began debating that question many months earlier, when Shawn and I had gathered the three boys around the oval kitchen table one evening. She and I have similar—and strong—opinions about the kinds of flashy, ostentatious affairs that have become commonplace, particularly in our part of Los Angeles. What should be meaningful coming-of-age rites have instead morphed into glitzy events centered around parties managed by professional event planners.

We knew we didn't want that.

At the same time, even the more toned-down celebrations at our relatively down-to-earth synagogue can prove stressful for the children who are marking the symbolic passage to adulthood. I have seen how some self-assured thirteen-year-olds relish the attention (Ami was one). For those who are less confident and more awkward in public situations, being the center of attention can induce panic and anxiety.

It's difficult to predict where Ezra might fall on that spectrum. It might not even occur to him to feel nervous. Yet his disregard for how people perceive his actions might prove severe. I can imagine my son spontaneously opting to recite the names of *Toy Story* characters instead of chanting his Torah portion, or even just exiting the room altogether—not out of rebellion, but because he doesn't perceive the occasion's importance. (I can recall several times when the buzz around a school performance or a play completely escaped Ezra's notice, while he paid acute attention to the movies—real or imaginary—playing out in his head.) All of that makes a bar mitzvah celebration for Ezra an unpredictable prospect.

Of course, we aren't making the decision in a vacuum. Our family belongs to a community that has its own customs. The medium-size chapel where we attend services most Saturday mornings is a comfortable and familiar place for Ezra, who has developed his own habits and routines. Early on, he spent time in the child-care program with a teen-age aide keeping an eye on him for safety. More recently he sits between Shawn and me in the pews of the chapel, flipping through the animal encyclopedias and *Simpsons* comic books he lugs to temple in his backpack. When he has reached his limit—usually thirty or forty minutes of a two-hour service—Ezra abruptly breaks for the door, then passes the rest of the morning happily pacing in the lobby. Only one time has Ezra endured an entire Shabbat-morning service: the day of his brother Ami's bar mitzvah. That sunny May morning, dressed in a navy blazer and white shirt, Ezra, then eleven, kept his eyes proudly locked on his older brother, not once attempting to slip out. Though he said little about it, his actions showed that he perceived the importance of the day.

That summer night in the kitchen, Shawn asks the boys what they think will be best for Ezra's bar mitzvah: a small, private ceremony so that Ezra is not overwhelmed? A service specially designed around him? A weekday ceremony, so that the crowd will be smaller?

"I don't understand why it's a question," Ami says.

Shawn explains that Ezra has a number of options, and that we want to choose the one most appropriate for him.

"He should just have a bar mitzvah," Noam says.

"He will," I explain. "We just want to hear from you what you think that should be like."

"He should do what every other kid does," Ami says. His tone carries a sense of defiance combined with pride in his brother.

"You don't think that would be hard for him?" I ask.

"He should do what I did and what every thirteen-year-old does," he repeats.

Noam agrees. It seems he has never even considered the question— has never pictured any other option.

Shawn asks Ezra what his preference is. He speaks up immediately.

"I want to have a bar mitzvah just like Ami," he says.

I glance at Shawn across the table. We share a silent look: Do we need to talk more? We know what our three sons want, and now we—and Ezra—have some work to do.

I understand without much discussion that Ezra's training will not be like anyone else's. Most twelve-year-olds in our community—already well versed in Hebrew language and the synagogue liturgy from years in Jewish day school or afternoon religious school—sign up with a tutor provided by the synagogue, who coaches them through a year or so of preparation. Ezra has picked up a rudimentary knowledge of Hebrew from Shawn's early instruction and several years in his after-school classes. And he has gained some mastery of the synagogue service at a Shabbat program for special-needs children at his Jewish summer camp,

another at the synagogue, and from many years of sitting in the congregation, listening even while he peruses his books.

Or so we hope.

It's his luck—or maybe his curse—to have a rabbi and a writer as his
parents. Shawn and I decide to split the tasks of preparing Ezra: She will
handle the synagogue liturgy, the Hebrew prayers, and passages from the
Torah he will chant for the community; I will help him compose his *d'var
Torah*, the speech the bar mitzvah boy traditionally delivers, commenting
on the week's biblical reading.

· It is difficult to imagine Ezra standing in one place long enough to
lead a Hebrew service. It is even harder to envision this boy—who so
assiduously avoids conversations—delivering much of a speech. Preparing Ezra will require—in addition to knowledge and persistence—
imagination.

Shawn is a talented and resourceful teacher, but I can't quite picture
how she is going to teach Ezra the seven verses from the biblical Book of
Numbers he will need to chant from the parchment scroll of the Torah—
a text in ancient Hebrew, without vowels or punctuation marks. I have
spent enough time sitting side by side with Ezra at our dining room table,
encouraging him through mathematics assignments and social studies
worksheets, to know his typical response to any kind of challenging
work: a deep groan, a declaration that, "It's too *haaaard*," and, often, a
tantrum.

But Shawn finds a way. Instead of setting a fixed weekly or daily time
to work with Ezra on the Torah reading, she intuitively follows his lead,
gauging his mood and energy, and fitting in lessons here and there, in the
ten or fifteen or twenty minutes Ezra is willing and able to focus. Like a
hunter stalking a deer, she carefully watches our son, somehow sensing

the right moments, seizing him, grabbing the photocopied Torah text we keep in a folder on a kitchen counter, and sitting down with him on a sofa to teach a new phrase. Shawn sings the Hebrew words, listening as Ezra repeats the phrases over and over and over. She uses every intuitive strength of Ezra's that works in his favor: impulsiveness, memory, melodic sense, willingness to repeat. For those few minutes, he repeats after her, adding a few words and musical notes at a time; then, when something inside him decides he's done, Ezra flees, speeding back to the computer screen or to cuddle with one of the cats.

Whenever he masters a new Hebrew verse, Shawn encourages him to demonstrate what he has learned for his brothers and me. Little by little, I watch and listen as—between videos and meals, homework, and all of the other things that occupy and distract Ezra—he gains a mastery of the material.

Watching Shawn and Ezra sneak off to the sofa or the kitchen table day after day, I begin to wonder how I will ever accomplish my part— helping him write his speech. Shawn reminds me frequently that I need to begin, but I let weeks and months pass without even making an attempt.

Part of my hesitation is that giving a speech is so different from anything Ezra has ever done. The other challenge is the material. The Torah portion that falls on Ezra's week happens to be a lengthy and dense section of Leviticus delineating how Israelite priests were to handle a variety of skin disorders. Ezra barely has the attention to follow a simple children's book. How am I going to interest him in a sober treatise on rashes of the ancient Middle East?

When I finally feel panicked enough to sit down with him—on a Sunday evening three months before the event—I try to show him a book that explains each Torah portion in simple language with images for children. I don't get far.

"I don't want to talk about *that*," he says.

I think he is simply having trouble understanding the content. I try to explain it again. Ezra bounces up from the couch and begins pacing the room.

"I don't want to talk about that," he repeats.

He doesn't mean that he doesn't want to discuss it with me right now; he means that he has no intention of giving a speech about skin diseases.

"But you're supposed to talk about the Torah," I tell him.

"I *do* want to talk about the Torah," Ezra says.

I start looking over the book again, searching for something to attract his interest.

Ezra keeps pacing. "I want to talk about God creating the world in seven days . . . and Adam and Eve . . . and the Garden of Eden . . . and the snake . . . and David and Goliath . . . and Moses and Pharaoh . . . and the Israelites leaving Egypt . . . and Mount Sinai . . . and the Ten Commandments. . . ."

He's free-associating, just the way he does about animals or Pixar characters. Only it's about the Torah. Ezra would keep going, but I stop him.

"Wait!" I say. "You're not going to talk about the *whole* Torah. You have to pick one part."

He keeps pacing. He looks frustrated, like he doesn't understand.

"I don't want to do it now," he says.

I tell him to think about it.

I realize part of my mistake: trying to get him to sit. Ezra usually focuses better when he's in motion. The next time I attempt to broach the subject, a few days later, I take him for a walk with Sasha. As we make our way through the neighborhood, I encourage him gently to focus more narrowly on what he wants to talk about in his speech. Finally, he comes up with an answer.

"I want to talk about me, Ezra," he says.

"What do you want to say?" I ask.

"I want to talk about being autistic," he says. "How it's not bad; it's good."

"You don't have to talk about that," I say.

"But I want to," he tells me.

"What do you want to say?"

"I want to say about memory and repeating," he says. "How I repeat a lot and how I have a very good memory."

I think of Tito, the Indian boy I met years earlier, and how I wondered at the time whether Ezra might ever be able to use words to describe his experience. Later, back home, we sit down as we have so many times, passing the laptop computer between us. Slowly, over time and over a few sessions, a text emerges, a story that only Ezra could tell.

As the day nears, I feel more and more anxious about the bar mitzvah. It isn't that I worry about Ezra learning the material. I have watched as he works with Shawn, adding one Hebrew phrase after another to the material he has mastered, until she can pull out the wrinkled photocopy of the *maftir*—the Torah selection he will be reading—and he can chant the entire selection spontaneously.

In the final weeks, we enlist the help of a family friend who will act as a shadow on the big day, in case Ezra needs extra assurance and direction. We set up a makeshift lectern in the dining room, where—when we can get his attention—Ezra practices his parts of the service and rehearses his speech. Shawn and I and his brothers listen and coach, gradually coaxing him to emphasize the words I have printed in bold and underlined on his pages of the talk.

"Slow down!" we keep telling him. "Remember: nice and loud!"

Part of my anxiety stems from my experience of my own bar mitzvah, some three decades earlier. That morning, I sat on the pulpit of the cavernous synagogue between the cantor and my grandfather, facing the congregation. In the middle of the service, forgetting that all eyes were on thirteen-year-old me, I signaled to my mother, seated in the front row, by pointing to my stomach with my right index finger, opening my mouth, and sticking out my tongue: international sign language for "I think I'm going to vomit." (I didn't.)

Yet there is something more than vicarious stage fright fueling my growing disquiet. In fact, Ezra's behavior can be so erratic that I feel certain he will surprise us in unforeseen ways when the day comes. Shawn and I have both assured Ezra that we will be proud of him no matter what happens—just for the efforts he has made.

What worries me is that Ezra won't show up. I am concerned that he will be physically at the synagogue, but that he won't be psychologically *present.* Even at thirteen, my son still spends so much of his day lost in his thoughts, focusing his mind's eye on the movies running in his head, that he often appears to miss what is transpiring in the real world directly around him. I tried to help eliminate some of his mental distractions when I showed him how to remove his obsessive thoughts about the gifts. Still, I worry that his bar mitzvah might turn into another version of his third birthday party, that morning a decade earlier when I found him in his bedroom conversing with Tigger, while the other toddlers played party games downstairs.

That is the concern that plays through my mind over and over as the day of Ezra's bar mitzvah nears: Will he show up?

I get the answer the instant I am awakened that Saturday morning. Sunlight is just creeping into our bedroom window when I feel the familiar sensation of the house vibrating and then hear the doorknob turn as Ezra dashes into our bedroom.

"It's the day of my bar mitzvah!" he is shouting over and over. Then louder: *"It's the day of my bar mitzvah!"* He is filled with unrestrained glee, greeting the day just as he celebrates the first day of every month, just as he marks the coming of each season, just as he leaps from bed when the long-awaited opening of a new animated movie arrives. He can hardly contain his zeal.

As quickly as he appeared, he disappears out the door. Shawn and I smile at each other, easing back into the bed until just a few minutes later, when Ezra bursts through the door again, already dressed in his gray suit pants, black dress shoes, and a crisp white shirt he is struggling to button at the cuffs.

It's six a.m. Three hours before we need to leave.

By the time we are close to the synagogue three hours later, Ezra's energy is reaching a crescendo. Always a fast walker, he is striding with determination half a block ahead of the rest of our family, dressed in his handsome dark gray suit, the familiar heavy red backpack full of his books strapped to his shoulders.

"You think he's nervous?" Ami asks.

"Excited," I say. "I don't think he gets nervous."

That is obvious the moment we arrive at the synagogue. Hundreds of times over the years, Ezra has walked through this same doorway, eyes to the floor or staring off, oblivious to the volunteers offering greetings as they extend their hands in welcome. Today, Ezra does something he has never done: Unprompted, he eagerly greets everyone in sight—an elderly lady applying rouge in the lobby, an early-arriving uncle, the security guard.

"Thank you!" he replies with exaggerated affect as they offer congratulations. "Thank you for *coming*!"

We make our way to the chapel. Only a handful of congregants have arrived as Shawn and I begin settling into a front pew—the special one for bar mitzvah families. Ezra won't sit, instead standing on tiptoe and peering around the room eagerly.

When I finally persuade him to sit, I unzip his backpack—almost from habit—and pull out one of the animal encyclopedias. I figure the distraction is the only guarantee to anchor him in place for the morning.

"Want to look at your book?" I ask him.

"No," he says, pushing my hand away. "I just want to look at my *bar mitzvah*."

He watches the stream of congregants and guests filing in through a rear door. Suddenly, he steps over me and then his brothers and out to the aisle. Shawn and I exchange a look. *Oh, no.* I assume this is his moment to flee for the lobby. Instead, he runs up to my uncle Les, who is in for the occasion from the East Coast. Ezra reaches for Les's hand and pumps it, smiling broadly and then moving on to the next person.

I just want to look at my bar mitzvah. Those words echo in my mind as the preliminary parts of the service begin and I watch Ezra make his way from one congregant to the next, smiling, chatting, receiving hugs and kisses.

"Thank you!" he keeps saying to each person, with that same awkwardly high volume and strong emphasis. "Thank you for *coming!*"

Watching him work the crowd—shaking hands and accepting kisses with only minimal fuss—I call to mind the little boy who wandered around his preschool classroom seeming to occupy his own world, a child so unmindful of other human beings that he would stumble into the other toddlers, not perceiving their existence. I think of the Ezra who once seemed incapable of looking me in the eye, who paced alone on the playground, whose mother wondered if he would ever say the words *I love you.*

Now that boy stands in his suit, fire-engine red bow tie, white knit yarmulke, and wire-framed glasses, smiling, confident, making his way through the carpeted aisles of the synagogue, warmly receiving each new face he encounters. He is the same Ezra—with his distinctive, awkward posture and the way he holds his long arms at his sides or tightly crossed on his chest—but he is soaking up the attention and the moment.

Eventually we are able to lure Ezra back to our row, where he takes a place to my right, with Shawn on his other side. Noam and Ami are beside us. Behind us sit our four parents—Ezra's grandparents—and our siblings, together with their own children. As the service proceeds, the rows behind us steadily fill until the chapel is far exceeding its capacity of more than three hundred: counselors from his summer camp, teachers from his school, neighbors and cousins and therapists. Still more file in as the prayers progress: invited guests, regular congregants, and curious onlookers dropping in from the synagogue's other Shabbat services stand shoulder-to-shoulder along the walls.

A moment before Ezra is to ascend to the podium to begin his part of the service, I extend an arm around his shoulders and look him over. My worry once was that he would not be able to arrive at this day with appropriate presence of mind. But he is here. Ezra is present in full force, in a way I have never seen, a way I have never imagined.

That becomes even clearer a few minutes later, when Shawn and I stand behind him as our family follows the Torah scroll in a processional through the aisles of the chapel. I watch Ezra extending his hand to greet one guest after another by name, with enthusiasm and delight. It seems he is connected to every soul in the room.

When it is time for him to chant his Torah reading, Ezra stands at the bimah and says the Hebrew blessings. Shawn and I stand on one side of him. He holds a silver Torah pointer, glances at the parchment Torah scroll laid out in front of him, and launches into chanting the seven biblical verses he has learned with Shawn over these many months. His chanting is flawless, confident and strong. When the pointer in his hand strays from the Hebrew words as he chants, Shawn tries to steer his hand back toward the correct place in the text, but Ezra stubbornly resists, pulling his hand away from hers, proceeding without hesitation through the biblical passage. It's as if he needs to make a statement: *You helped me to get here, but I'm going to do this on my own.* His eyes don't appear to be focusing on the scroll; his gaze seems to be on the hundreds of people gathered around him at that moment. (A friend in the congregation later describes it this way: Ezra wasn't reciting the words from the scroll or from memory, but rather from a Torah that seemed to exist in his mind.)

When he finishes, dozens of men and women suddenly emerge from their seats, join hands, and dance a hora around Ezra, who stands between Shawn and me, a radiant smile spreading across his face, showing joy, surprise, and relief all at once.

A few minutes later, he steps back up to the podium, takes an exaggerated, deep breath, and launches into his speech, the one he has written, with my support, over our walks and tag-team sessions passing the laptop:

Shabbat shalom.

It is finally my bar mitzvah. I have worked for many months and now it's here at last.

Today in the Torah we read a *parsha* called Tazria-Metzora. It has lots of information about skin diseases and what happens when mold grows on your house. I decided that instead of talking about that, I want to tell you about some of my favorite parts of the Torah. I have three favorite parts.

My favorite Torah portion is the story of Noah. The Torah says there were a lot of evil people in the world, so God told Noah that God was going to make a flood. Noah built an ark. It was gigantic. I like that story because it includes a lot of animals: elephants, giraffes, lions, zebras, hippos, and a lot more. Probably even my favorite animals, lemurs and otters. If I were Noah, I wouldn't have wanted the flood to end. Then I could have just stayed on the ark with the animals.

Another story I love in the Torah is about David and Goliath. David was a little boy who heard that there was a giant named Goliath who worked for the Philistines. David was just a little boy. But he had a slingshot and he shot a rock at

Goliath and killed him. That was a miracle. David showed that even though you might be small, you can still have a lot of power.

My other favorite story is about Moses. I remember when my uncle dressed as Pharaoh on Passover 2003, when I was seven years old. I felt a bit scared. The real Moses must have been even more scared of the real Pharaoh. But God helped Moses by making the plagues. Ten of them: blood, frogs, lice, wild beasts, cattle disease, boils, hail, locusts, darkness, and the slaying of the firstborn. Finally Pharaoh let the Israelites go. I like that story because it was a miracle that the Israelites were finally free.

In all my favorite parts of the Torah, God makes miracles. And today feels like a miracle too. I am finally thirteen years old. So let me tell you about me. I am an autistic person. That means that my brain works differently than other people's brains. Sometimes I repeat things when I don't mean to. Sometimes it's hard to focus in school.

Sometimes autism is very helpful. One good thing is that I have a very good memory. I still remember my first day of preschool at the Hungry Caterpillar class at Temple Isaiah with my teacher, Dawn. I also remember when I went to my bubbe and grandpa's beach house in Arch Cape, Oregon, when I was a baby, and I liked to sit and throw rocks in the creek for hours and hours. I remember when my *savta* and papa took me to a farm in Kentucky when I was seven and we met Farmer Frank and his cranky goose.

I like to remember things I enjoy, such as Disney movie running times and release dates. Did you know that *101 Dalmatians* is seventy-nine minutes long and it was released on January twenty-fifth, 1961? Or did you know that *The Jungle Book* is seventy-eight minutes long, and it came out on October eighteenth, 1967? That's the same day our friend Deborah was born. My bubbe was born in 1937, the same year as *Snow White and the Seven Dwarfs*. Walt Disney was born in 1901 and died in 1966. He was only sixty-five but he had a wonderful life. So I remember him too.

I also remember all kinds of facts about dogs. I know which breeds are friendly and which ones are unfriendly, which ones are utility dogs, which ones are hounds, and which ones are terriers, and many more. I get excited when I meet people who have dogs. I like to tell them all about what makes their dog special.

So, you see, it helps to have a good memory.

Sometimes I think that all Jewish people are autistic. Jews repeat things all the time. And Jews have a very good memory.

We repeat Shabbat every week. And we sing the same songs, like "Shalom Aleichem" and "Adon Olam" and the Kiddush.

And we also have holidays that help us remember things that happened thousands of years ago. On Pesach we remember the Jews getting out of Egypt. On Purim, we remember Queen Esther. And we also have sad holidays. On Tisha B'av we don't eat because we're sad that the temple in Jerusalem got destroyed thousands of years ago.

We remember all these things. That's part of being Jewish.

But today, on the day of my bar mitzvah, we celebrate a different kind of holiday. When I chanted from the Torah today it was the *maftir* for Rosh Chodesh, the first day of the month of Iyar. Rosh Chodesh is a Jewish holiday that isn't about something that happened a long time ago. Rosh Chodesh is the beginning of a new month. It's not about remembering the past. Rosh Chodesh is about remembering the future.

Today we are celebrating the future. That's why it's a great day to be celebrating my becoming bar mitzvah. I do have a great memory of the past—but today is about my great future.

Thank you for being here to help me celebrate my future.

When he finishes, the congregation greets him with spontaneous applause and cheers—not common reactions in synagogue on Shabbat morning, but people can't restrain their emotions. Many are wiping away tears. I hold Shawn's hand and choke up. It isn't so much the words as the way he said them that has created a transcendent moment. His sweetness, the awkward way he emphasized words, his unfiltered and unrestrained enthusiasm—these reveal a genuine quality in Ezra one rarely experiences in teenagers or, really, in anyone.

Shawn and I step to the podium and stand on either side of our son to share our own thoughts for the occasion. Shawn talks about his name, Ezra Moshe, and how it is all about the Torah: His middle name is Moshe, Hebrew for Moses, who received the Torah at Mount Sinai. Ezra, the Hebrew prophet, was reputed to have written it all down. She talks about the part of the day's Torah portion Ezra opted not to discuss, the passage detailing skin disorders among ancient Israelite priests.

"A lot of people are uncomfortable with this part of the Torah," she says. "It's about people who have a condition, for unknown reasons, that makes life hard and challenging for them and changes the way the community treats them. In our family we know very well what that's like—to struggle with something that is challenging—personally, to the family and to the community."

I tell a story. Recently we were in a restaurant in the neighborhood, and Ezra introduced himself to a woman at the next table. When she asked the meaning of his name, he told her that the word *ezra* in Hebrew means "help." Then he told her something I had never heard before. "My parents gave me that name when I was a baby because when I grow up, I'm going to help them."

"Ezra," I say, "you have already helped us."

At the luncheon following the service, I stand with Ezra and Shawn as she publicly welcomes the guests in the synagogue's airy ballroom and then acknowledges a long list of people who have helped Ezra along the way: Dave, the gym teacher; Dawn, the preschool aide; his teachers and therapists; his grandparents; Ami and Noam. While she offers thanks and guests eat their bagels and pasta salad, Ezra crosses his arms and paces in little circles beside us, eyes on his shiny black shoes and the hardwood dance floor.

The music picks up, and the crowd sweeps Ezra to the center of the floor, where a small circle of family and friends begins dancing around him. That group becomes two, then three, then four concentric circles of loved ones, arms linked in another dance. Ezra raises his hands over his head and jumps on his toes. The boy who once seemed so alone, who has fled for years from human contact, spreads his arms, fingers extended, bouncing on his toes as his brothers, his parents, his grandparents, and dozens upon dozens of friends surround him with an ecstatic communal embrace.

Years before, we frequently came to this very ballroom on Shabbat afternoons after services for receptions just like this one. Back then, Ezra was so sensitive to the noise, his senses so overwhelmed by the crowds, that he would linger at the doorway; dashing in with both hands cupped over his ears to muffle the roar of the crowd, he would grab a fistful of cookies, then scurry outside to sit alone eating his treats. For a second, a thought strikes me: Now that same boy is jumping in ecstasy just a few rooms away from the synagogue's preschool, the place where, a decade earlier, Shawn and I crammed our bodies into toddler-size chairs to hear a teacher explain something about our middle son: He wasn't like the other children.

How right she was.

Back in My Brain

Nine days after the celebration, on an ordinary Monday afternoon, I am at the computer in my home office when I hear the squeaking brakes that always announce the arrival of Ezra's yellow school bus. I peek out my office window and catch a glimpse of my son, red backpack slung over his shoulders, jogging up the front walk in the sunshine.

I hear the front door swing open and the rapid footsteps as Ezra dashes into the house. Almost every day that sound is followed by the slam of his knapsack hitting the hardwood foyer floor and then his sprint to the den and the computer. Today is different.

"Abba?" I hear him shout.

"Hi, Ez!" I call back.

A moment later, he's at my office door.

"Abba!" Ezra says quickly. "We forgot to go to Beverly Drive!"

"What?"

"I remembered something: We forgot to go back and get the lump on Beverly Drive!"

I smile, amazed that he has remembered our talk from a couple of weeks earlier, and even more impressed that he has let it go for a week. (Of course, it helps that he has already used a few gift cards to acquire the coveted three-volume *Star Wars* set.)

"When should we go?" I ask.

"We have to go *now*," Ezra says.

I slip the leash onto Sasha, and we head out the door. Ezra, in blue jeans and a navy T-shirt, strides rapidly twenty or thirty feet ahead of me. I hold the leash of the dog, who is trotting to keep up with Ezra, following him as he makes the turn to the left, onto wide and tree-lined Beverly Drive. I trail the two of them, watching boy and dog bound up the boulevard a few blocks until we are approaching the familiar spot.

"Where is it?" I call to Ezra.

"Over there!" Ezra says, pointing up ahead.

I play along. "I don't think it's here," I say. "It's a little bit farther."

Ezra runs to a spot in the grass.

"Over a little," I say, pointing. He moves. "There! I see it!"

He leans over, pantomimes grabbing something off the ground, then slaps his right palm to his ear, as if he's shoving something into his head. He makes a whooshing sound, blowing air through pursed lips.

"Back in my brain," he says.

I nod, smiling. "I'm proud of you," I say.

He turns around, grabs the leash from me, and heads back toward home, picking up right where he left off two weeks earlier. With his dog at his side, he walks and chatters about *Star Wars* books, gift cards, and the new book he has in mind, an illustrated guide to reptiles. And I follow Ezra home.

ACKNOWLEDGMENTS

I am grateful to my son Ezra for allowing me to tell his story, and for his cheerful assistance along the way. When I couldn't quite pinpoint when a particular event occurred, I would ask him. "That was in April of 2004," he'd say, "a Sunday, three weeks after the release of Disney's *Home on the Range*." If you ever consider writing a memoir, I highly recommend enlisting the help of someone with a superhuman memory.

I also suggest a talented agent, and I was privileged to find one in the remarkable Betsy Amster. She was an enthusiastic champion and cheerleader, even joining Ezra and me on a memorable visit to the Oregon Zoo, where she showed good humor in following Ezra . . . into the bat exhibit.

I am indebted to Tracy Bernstein, whose skillful editing and guidance greatly improved every page. Tiffany Yates offered meticulous copyediting, Mimi Bark created a cover with exactly the joy and whimsy I hoped for, and Alissa Amell designed the pages with flair.

This is a family story, and I am blessed to have a supportive and nurturing clan. My parents, Lora and Jim Meyer—to whom I dedicate this book—never fail to overwhelm me with their generosity, thoughtfulness, and wisdom. Sandey and Del Fields, my loving in-laws, consistently backed and cheered my efforts and helped on the home front when I headed off for writing retreats. The four of them are exemplary grandparents to Ezra and his brothers, as well as topnotch researchers: A week rarely passes without one of them pointing me to a new article or broadcast about autism.

Many parts of this book had their origins in pieces I wrote in Kelly Morgan's writing workshop. I am grateful for Kelly's gift of gently coaxing creativity and I thank the members of her Thursday night group for their helpful comments. Thanks, too, to Christopher Noxon, Tracy Miller, and Laura Slovin for honest and helpful critiques.

I had written about hundreds of families for *People* magazine when a colleague there, Patrick Rogers, suggested that I write about my own. The resulting article became the seed of this book, and I am indebted to Patrick as well as Betsy Gleick and Larry Hackett for their fine editing and support.

I was fortunate to enlist the talents of four friends, each of whom offered thoughtful and thorough editing of an early draft. Trudy Ames, Tom Booth, Mary Hanlon, and Andrea King went above and beyond to help me find the heart of the story and make the pages sing. I cannot thank them enough for their efforts. Bruce Frankel offered valuable advice and moral support in the homestretch.

Many people provided quiet space to work when I needed it. For the gift of solitude, I am obliged to David Myers of UCLA; Chris and Darrell Cozen; and Jennifer and Daniel Greyber and Camp Ramah in California.

I have gained insight and perspective about my son from many of the caring professionals who have worked with him over the years, among them: Dr. Ricki Robinson, Esther Hess, Dave Rabb, Dawn Farber, Sharon Asarch, Elaine Hall, Mara Fiore, Amira Hanna, Camp Ramah in California's Tikvah staff, and Amit Bernstein and Howie Hoffman of Media Enrichment Academy. From early on, Elana Artson provided valuable advice and wisdom.

I am grateful to Temple Beth Am and the members of its Library Minyan for providing a home every Saturday morning where Ezra can peruse his animal books amid warmth and prayer.

My sons Ami and Noam are extraordinary brothers, sons, and individuals. I benefited from Ami's excellent wording and design suggestions, and Noam proved to be an eagle-eyed proofreader. I thank them both for their patience and for their excitement about this project. Ami and Noam are growing to become exactly what Shawn and I tell them each day to be: mensches.

People often ask me what you're supposed to call the husband of a rabbi. My answer: lucky. No words can express my gratitude to Shawn, who has shared every step of this journey. She has been unwavering in her faith in me, her encouragement, and her willingness to listen carefully as I created this book. Shawn frequently exhorts her students to "do a close reading of the text." That's exactly what she did to this one, and in the process she helped to make it much better. More important, she brings meaning, light, love, and laughs to every day.